Africa south of the Sahara is undergoing a species of social as well as industrial revolution, and one of the most striking characteristics of this phenomenon is urbanization. Taking sub-Saharan Africa as an example, this book seeks to show the general significance of urbanization for social change in developing regions of the world. Urbanization is treated as a social process and the study focuses primarily on the sociology of urban population growth rather than on urbanism *per se*.

Professor Little distinguishes between the 'traditional' and the 'modern' town, and describes how the latter has come into being. He deals with attitudes to wage employment and the modern town's social structure, and discusses the implications for it of 'class' and 'ethnicity'. Other bases of social organization, such as family, social networks and voluntary associations, are also described, and the connection between urbanization and race relations is explained. A final chapter considers the advantages and disadvantages of using an urban concept for purposes of analysing the contemporary development of African society.

Kenneth Little is Professor of African Urban Studies in the University of Edinburgh. He has held the post of Visiting Professor at a number of universities, including Ghana, Khartoum, California, Fisk, New York, Northwestern and Washington. Professor Little's previous publications include *Negroes in Britain* (1948, revised edition 1972) and *The Mende of Sierra Leone* (1951, revised edition 1967), both published by Routledge & Kegan Paul, and two books specifically concerned with the present work's topic — *West African Urbanization* (1965) and *African Women in Towns* (1973), published by Cambridge University Press.

Urbanization as a social process

Library of Man

Edited by Adam Kuper
Department of Anthropology
University College London

Also in this series

Aylward Shorter　*East African Societies*

A catalogue of social science books published by Routledge & Kegan Paul will be found at the end of this volume.

Urbanization as a social process

An essay on movement and change in contemporary Africa

Kenneth Little

Professor of African Urban Studies
University of Edinburgh

Routledge & Kegan Paul
London and Boston

First published in 1974
by Routledge & Kegan Paul Ltd
Broadway House, 68–74 Carter Lane,
London EC4V 5EL and
9 Park Street,
Boston, Mass. 02108, USA
Set in Linotype Times
and printed in Great Britain by
Willmer Brothers Limited, Birkenhead

ISBN 0 7100 7931 1 (c)
ISBN 0 7100 7932 X (p)
Library of Congress Catalog Card No. 74 - 80750

Contents

Acknowledgments

I wish to thank Professor A. L. Epstein and the editors of the *Rhodes-Livingstone Journal* for permission to quote excerpts from his article entitled 'The Network and Urban Social Organization'. I have also to thank Mrs Elizabeth Mandeville and Dr Barbara Harrell-Bond for permission to draw on their unpublished work and the Addison-Wesley Publishing Company, Inc., Reading, Massachusetts, for allowing me to reprint nearly two pages of demographic data and to include, in a slightly different form, some portions of my Module, 'Some Aspects of African Urbanization South of the Sahara'.

In addition, my sincere thanks are also due to the Trustees of the Noel Buxton Trust and to the Trustees of the Carnegie Trust for the Universities of Scotland for the financial assistance they most kindly contributed. This helped substantially with the necessary research and preparation of this book.

Kenneth Little

Edinburgh

Urban life does not draw relatives apart, it draws them together. In our country brothers quarrel over land and property; but in the town there is none to quarrel over and they come to each other for protection.

(Statement by a Luo migrant in Kampala, quoted by Marguerite Jellicoe, 1968, p.7.)

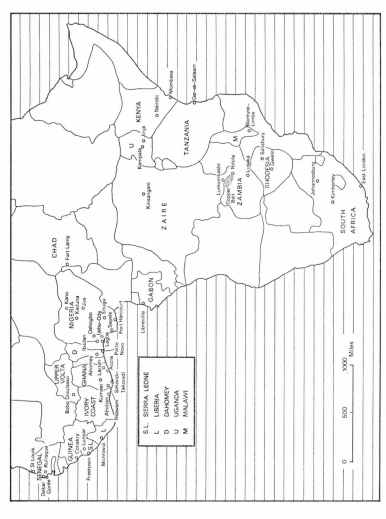

Map *Principal towns discussed in the text*

Introduction

I have written this book for two interrelated reasons. First, I believe that the *empirical* basis of social anthropological methods of study is worth preserving. This is going to be increasingly difficult if the so-called primitive social systems continue to be the main focus of attention and research. True, there are some parts of the world where, isolated from outside contact by mountain ranges and deep forest, small indigenous populations still follow an immemorial way of life. But situations of this kind in, for example, the more remote areas of New Guinea and Brazil, are now relatively rare; and it is very much more common to find that traditional cultures have been penetrated and influenced at nearly all their most strategic points by industrialization and other 'modernizing' forces. Nor does even a high rate of illiteracy necessarily betoken the persistence of traditional forms of social organization.

It so happened that my own first spell of fieldwork in Africa was begun at the end of 1944. At this time, among the Mende people I was studying, rather less than 5 per cent of children of school age received any education at all, compared with about 1 per cent in the Sierra Leone Protectorate as a whole. Despite this and the virtual absence, apart from Freetown, of towns of a 'modern' kind, it was immediately clear that several important sectors of upcountry life bore little correspondence to conditions during the pre-colonial era. True, once one left the single-track railway connecting Freetown with the hinterland, one found – as is still largely the case today – that the traditional organization of kinship was relatively intact; but a large part of the political and legal system was new.

It had been virtually created by the colonial government through the setting up of native authorities. These involved the placing of all rulers of chiefdoms on the same footing, whereas, prior to the inauguration of the Protectorate, 'high chiefs' were differentiated from lesser chiefs. In other words, under 'indigenous' conditions there were among the Mende and other peoples outside colonial jurisdiction several small hegemonies which were headed by the more successful warrior chiefs to whom subordinate rulers owed fealty. Moreover, unlike the situation 'frozen' by pacification, shifts in the balance of power were, apparently, quite frequent, and a given high chief's ability to dominate his neighbours was bound up extensively with the relationship between secular administration and certain supposedly supernatural agencies, notably the Poro secret society. Such a situation being obviously incompatible with European methods of administration, Poro activities were declared illegal. This deprived the association of any 'official' political role but not of the part it continued to play 'underground'.

A further change introduced by the British was that the chiefs, as officers of the native authority, were paid emoluments instead of being entitled, as was customary, to chiefdom labour and to deal in slaves. Also, not only were chiefs now 'elected' on a basis of semi-popular candidature, but legal procedure in the native administration courts was on 'European' lines. In other words, evidence was heard by the chief and his 'big men' who decided on the verdict, the whole set-up being somewhat similar to the magistracy in Britain. However, 'in the old days', I was told, it was not the 'bench' but the witnesses to the case who collectively arrived at judgment after 'hanging heads' together, rather in the manner of a modern jury. In addition, plaintiff and defendant were allowed to back up their respective pleas not only by calling witnesses, but by staking quantities of property, including slaves. Each tried to out-bid the other and the loser forfeited everything he had deposited (Little, 1965–6, *passim*; and 1967b, pp. 40–1, 176–7, 202–4).

This information about the pre-colonial political system and its legal procedures was given me by elderly informants who were young men in the days prior to British rule. What they told me helped me to 'reconstruct' an interesting aspect of the Mende's traditional heritage. Nevertheless, it raises the question of an investigator's technical position. If, instead of being able to check a reported situation for himself, he is obliged to rely on the memories of senile or near-senile informants, is he really working as an anthropologist at all?

2

Such methodological problems are the more important because since the 1940s a great deal of social change has taken place throughout Africa, especially following Independence. Consequently, if it was difficult *empirically* to study 'traditional society' in a relatively 'untouched' corner of Africa nearly thirty years ago, how much greater must be the obstacles today? Certainly, there are very good reasons indeed for recording everything that can possibly be learned about African society at the pre-contact stage. But there is also an equal need to be realistic and this means taking increasingly into account trends which Godfrey Wilson perceived as early as 1941. He wrote then (p. 12):

Today the inhabitants of Northern Rhodesia are members of a huge world-wide community, and their lives are bound up at every point with the events of its history. New methods of transport by bicycle, lorry and rail have increased their own range of travel twentyfold. Many of them now seek a European language, and most of them have learnt the language of some other tribe than their own. European employers, rulers and ministers of religion link them to the life of the world. Their standard of living now depends on economic conditions in Europe, Asia, and America to which continents their labour has become essential. Their political development is largely decided in the Colonial Office and on the battlefields of Europe; while hundreds of their one-time separate tribes now share a single destiny. Many of them, as Christians, look for religious organisations and guidance to the Vatican, to English and American bishops and to Free Church synods, and accept dogmas and moral rules of universal application. They have entered a heterogeneous world stratified into classes and divided into states, and so find themselves suddenly transformed into the peasants and un-skilled workers of a nascent nation state.

I shall be elaborating on Wilson's thesis in my final chapter, but for immediate purposes it will suffice to stress two things. First, Wilson foresaw that one of the most important features of African life was going to be the movement of people into towns. Second, he indicated what there is still some reluctance to concede, namely, that for practical purposes anthropologists would need to conduct such research within conceptual frameworks capable of accommodating large-scale social systems. Wilson's own fieldwork and

3

that of his successors, Clyde Mitchell, Max Gluckman, A. L. Epstein, Philip Mayer and other more recent writers, has been salutary in this regard. It has pointed the way ahead, and shown that there is, in fact, fresh scope for anthropology's most important method. This – to repeat – is the direct study of human society through observation/participation, carried on now within contexts of movement and change.

It is for the above reasons, then, that the theme of this book is urbanization. Its approach is in essay form because, in my view, the provision of a single formula for the study of African social change is, as yet, premature. Since, moreover, the intention here is merely to explore this concept's use for heuristic purposes, I have tried to move cautiously and without ambiguity.

This is necessary because authors employ 'urbanization' in several different ways. It frequently refers, for example, to living in towns as against living in rural settlements, and it is with this meaning that simple quantitative indices of urbanization are some-times constructed. Thus, the 1960 Census of Ghana defined localities having more than 5,000 residents as urban, and in an often-quoted article Bascom has pointed out that in Western Nigeria the estimated index of urbanization falls between that of the USA and Canada. He calculated that the distribution of population in Yoruba urban centres is very similar to that of France. The difficulty about such a measure is that it indicates the proportion of the population living in cities, but it throws no light upon the rate at which the cities have grown (Bascom, 1955, pp. 446–54; Epstein, 1967, p. 270). Another type of definition holds that urbanization is a process of population concentration in which the ratio of urban people to the total population in a territory increases. This defini-tion implies a definition of cities independent of the process of urban growth, and 'from this point of view an increase both in the size of the individual points of concentration and in the number of points of urban concentration may occur without an increase in the urbanization of a territory. Only when a larger proportion of the inhabitants in an area come to live in the cities is urbanization said to occur' (Reiss, 1964, p. 739).

Since the social life of cities is undoubtedly affected and influenced by demographic factors, all the above definitions are relevant to sociological analysis. On their own, however, they explain little or nothing about the way in which relationships are organized, and so my employment of 'urbanization' is different. As will be explained briefly in Chapter 1, I use it to refer wholly and specifically to social process in a somewhat similar sense to the definition of Wirth (1938), and even more closely to that of Clyde Mitchell. The former author speaks of urbanization in terms of the cumulative accentuation of characteristics distinctive of the mode of life associated with the growth of cities. Mitchell refers to the process of becoming urban, moving to cities, changing from agriculture to other pursuits common to cities, and corresponding changes of behaviour patterns (quoted in Breese, 1966, p. 3).

The advantage of the latter kind of definition is that it enables a distinction to be made between the social effects and implications of rapid increases in city size and the way of life of people inhabiting cities. This distinction is particularly necessary in the present context because, as the text will explain, most African urban populations are both unstable and continuously adding to their numbers, principally through immigration. What, therefore, the analyst has to deal with is the sociology of urban population growth rather than patterns of urbanism *per se*. Urbanization, used non-sociologically, measures the difference between the two situations in demographic terms but throws no direct light upon the social processes involved.

Another problem is that the demographic and the sociological meanings of urbanization are sometimes employed interchangeably, thereby creating ambiguity. Breese, whose useful book raises this point, himself distinguishes between 'physical urbanization' and 'social urbanization'. By the former term he means *where* people live; and, by the latter, the provision of appropriate amenities for urban life (p. 100). But this appropriate and logical suggestion does not prevent Breese himself speaking of urbanization in terms of the percentage of urban populations and then using the expression a few paragraphs later to describe the development of 'delegative, representative governments' (pp. 4–5).

In the latter case Breese is obviously referring to 'social structure', and so I myself have deliberately substituted some such phrase as 'urban population growth' for 'urbanization' except where questions of social process are *specifically* involved. This, admittedly, is a somewhat cumbersome procedure; but it makes for consistency and is, I submit, less likely to confuse sociological with demographic issues. It is, therefore, on this terminological basis that the argument will be laid and will proceed in the succeeding chapters.

I

The migratory basis of urban growth

Africa south of the Sahara is undergoing a species of social as well as industrial revolution and one of the most striking characteristics of this phenomenon is urbanization. By urbanization is meant the process whereby people acquire material and non-material elements of culture, behaviour patterns and ideas that originate in or are distinctive of the city. African urbanization is the more remarkable because at the present time less than 10 per cent of the continent's population live in cities of 100,000 or more inhabitants (Davis, 1968, p. 38).

The reason for this slow start is that in the thousand years before any serious penetration by Europeans began, the basic social structure changed very little. This was the case though peoples conquered and peoples moved, though extra-continental influences filtered over the Sahara and up the Nile and touched the coast. In fact, an essentially African pattern of society, organized more often than not into essentially African states, was in existence, and included the empires of Ghana, Mali, Songhai, the Hausa states and Kanem-Bornu as the outstanding examples. This was long before any contact with Christianity or Islam was possible, although in due course these Sudanic states came in touch across the desert with the Arab civilization of North Africa. Ambassadors from North African sultanates and Moslem scholars, too, frequently travelled with the merchants who plied these caravan roads of the Sahara (cf. Oliver and Atmore, 1967, *passim*; Bovill, 1933, *passim*; *et al.*).

But south of the Sahara, Africa was little affected by the outside world until the present century. This applies even to South Africa, where diamonds were discovered at Kimberley in 1869 and gold on the Witwatersrand in 1884. However, only during and after the First

7

and Second World Wars did South Africa experience the economic reorganization that transformed an agrarian society into an industrial one. In the West Coast, Africans had been in contact with Europe for several centuries, but European settlement and political control was confined virtually to the littoral and the strip of land behind it until well on into the nineteenth century. The Western impact was signifcant only in specific ways, for example, in stimulating intertribal warfare and local trading in slaves. Commerce with Europeans was mostly on terms of equality, and in the interior it was conducted by barter, a 'bar' serving as a standard of value; European currency circulated only in some places on the coast itself. By and large, therefore, the structure of West African society remained on a non-monetary, subsistence or semi-subsistence basis. Elsewhere, there was white settlement in limited areas but with the exception of European mining operations and farming the situation was similar (Little, 1953, pp. 274–5).

What altered the entire picture was the European partition of Africa. This colonization took place on an almost continental scale and African life was invaded by Western economic enterprise and its market economy. These capitalist interests required urban facilities which previously had barely existed and so, in West Africa, for example, British and French settlements at such places as Accra, Freetown, Dakar and Lagos were developed as entrepôts. Later, Enugu grew in response to nearby coalfields, and Port Harcourt was created in turn as a terminus for a railway bringing coal from Enugu to the coast. Upcountry towns – some of them, like Kumasi, the capitals of ancient kingdoms – gained their *raison d'être* as modern cities through developing as centres for communications and collecting points for locally-produced commodities such as cocoa, groundnuts and palm kernels. In many other places the extraction of minerals, including gold, diamonds, iron ore and tin, was extensively undertaken.

Naturally, workers were needed to provide labour and services for these various economic enterprises, although at first the idea made little appeal to the ordinary villager. Working for money and wage-labour was foreign to the tribesman of the late nineteenth century. It savoured somewhat of slavery. Usually, he had resources of his own, showed little interest in the trade goods procurable by money, and so had little desire to earn it. In consequence, there was a desperate shortage of labour for modern enterprise, especially in the territories under British control. There, although opposed to Africans being directly forced into wage-labour, the government imposed taxes which had to be paid in cash. This had the desired effect because in the absence of marketable crops or produce the money demanded could only be obtained by working for it. Nyasaland Africans, for example, were made to labour on public works until they had earned an equivalent, while labour was secured directly for the South African mines through recruitment in Nyasaland and Northern Rhodesia as well as in South Africa itself (Mitchell, 1962, pp. 196–200). In western Africa, where the population of the interior was regarded as a potential source of labour, the French drew especially upon the Mossi of the Upper Volta.

Mossi migrants found that working in the Gold Coast was more profitable than trade because they were paid in coins that could be exchanged for French money. But the taxes were raised gradually, obliging more and more Mossi men to migrate, and those men who were unwilling or unable to obtain European money with which to pay taxes had their goods sequestrated and sold. The Mossi also bore the brunt of the French demand for labour after the First World War and their chiefs were made to recruit tens of thousands of their subjects both for public works and for private commercial enterprises (Skinner, 1965, pp. 60–6). In the Belgian Congo, forced labour was officially prohibited but when attempts to attract workers to the copper and gold mines failed, the government supported the mine-owners' recruiting drives. A circular of 1922, for example, emphasized the duty of helping private enterprise when necessary; and, to quote the officialese, 'if moral authority, encouragement and favour failed, marks of displeasure were to be imposed'. The state itself had large interests in most of the industrial enterprises concerned; and so, in the diplomatic language of Hailey's *African Survey* (1939, pp. 644–5), 'local officers gave an effective compliance' to these instructions, thereby enabling large numbers of African workers to be 'recruited'.

These direct and indirect methods of obliging Africans to migrate did not in themselves establish a wholly new pattern. Some peoples already had a tradition of rendering labour to their chiefs, and others accepted that, having been militarily defeated, they had to obey. Moreover, many migrations of African peoples transpired long before the advent of colonialism. These often involved movements resulting from military conquest and the flight of war refugees from their own tribal land to safer places. There was, for example, the Fulani expansion in West Africa and the Luba-Lunda extension into what are now Zaire and Angola. Indian migration to Zanzibar and the coastal regions of East Africa went on from 1830 to 1890; and the Ndebele moved from Zululand to Rhodesia in 1837 and Sotho groups to Botswana and the Transvaal.[1] In addition, many migrations have been caused or motivated by the need to find a more favourable environment when there was insect and disease infestation, and very considerable movements which have continued to take place as people have moved to seek new lands either for subsistence purposes or for the planting of cash crops (Colson, 1960, pp. 60–1).[2]

What, however, altered the traditional situation, sociologically, was the introduction, through labour migration, of money. Previously, some currencies such as cowrie shells were locally employed, but money in a European form was virtually unknown upcountry. Indeed, when English gold sovereigns first appeared in the hinterland of Sierra Leone they were treated as curiosities, people played with them as if they were marbles, and silver coins were melted down for ornaments (Alldridge, 1910). The difference now was that tribesmen who earned money were able to exchange it for European manufactured goods and local producers who had previously bartered or made a more or less direct exchange of their palm kernels for Manchester cloths were now paid in cash. All this extended the use of money as a standard value, and it was gradually employed in an increasing number of transactions, including social ones, with fellow tribesmen. This required that a monetary medium of exchange be introduced into further corners of the traditional life, and it meant that to an increasing extent an individual's livelihood must derive from the sale of something and must be regarded as resulting from sale (Little, 1953, p. 89). True, subsistence continued to provide most of the things required for daily life and at a pinch could produce everything essential. However, as the use of money grew and spread, it came to be seen as a special commodity necessary to exchange for certain goods which could not be manufactured in the rural village – chiefly clothing, blankets, household utensils, bicycles and guns. These things were not regarded as essential at the start but returning migrants from the town helped to make them popular. They thus became increasingly a part of local life, indispensable to the art of 'civilized' living.

The result was that migration for purposes of earning money became established as a voluntary procedure, especially as cash was now acceptable in place of the customary marriage payments. This made it possible for a young man who was enterprising enough, to obtain a wife for himself without depending upon father or relatives. Also, since money could be substituted for goods and services it became a preferred form of gift to relatives and friends. In any relationship in which gifts were exchanged, a small present of money was considered to be the most appropriate, and the chief, too, expected presents of money from his followers. What also made a regular supply of money important was the growing independence of women and their attitude towards marriage. For example, even in the 1940s there was a growing preference in Sierra Leone for men who were paid by the week or by the month; girls were less interested in farmers whose money came in once or twice during the year (Little, 1967b, pp. 166–7).

Money needed for these various purposes can be most readily earned in the industrialized areas and this explains why migration is mostly to the towns. Although it is mainly the younger men who are involved, numbers of unattached women and girls also move from the rural areas and some of the male migrants are accompanied by wives. The employers' demand is principally for unskilled labour; but the Africans realize that there are more favourable opportunities of earning a living if one has an education; and to be educated improves a person's social standing. There is another reason why young people move townwards, because few secondary schools and facilities for technical training exist outside the main towns and government offices and business establishments are also located there. Not only does this make urban residence virtually essential for the educated classes in general, but it brings in nearly everyone who is looking for advancement, especially in 'white-collar' forms of employment. Also, people in the villages sometimes send their sons and daughters to urban relatives to be taught a trade or 'minded' while at school, and traders come in to replenish their stock. The fact that there are frequently kinsfolk at hand to receive and house the migrant naturally enhances the town's attraction (cf. Balandier, 1955, pp. 203–8; Little, 1965, pp. 20–3; *et al.*).

Migration has also been encouraged by the very diversification of the economy,[3] as well as by the growing demand on the world market for locally grown products such as cocoa, groundnuts, cotton, sisal, etc. This, by stimulating the growth of cash crops, gave monetary value to land. It meant among some peoples that the older men were no longer prepared, as traditionally, to relinquish their land rights in favour of the younger generation and so the latter were obliged to move in search of other opportunities. This happened among the Nyakusa of Tanzania; and in Kenya, too, it has been found that the majority of the young men who migrated were landless and almost half of these landless men had no prospect of obtaining land unless they could earn money to purchase it (Gulliver, 1958, p. 2).

A further 'push' factor in migration was the increased pressure of population upon land resources. This occurred largely because technological developments in terms of improved health facilities and child-care led to a general growth in population without there always being an accompanying rise in food production. On the contrary, quite often indigenous methods of cultivation continued to be practised with a shorter and shorter period of fallow. This, by reducing the fertility of the soil, brought an overall decrease in the margin of subsistence and the density of population which the land could support. Hunger therefore provided another reason for migration because the absence of a large number of men away for several months went a considerable way towards conserving supplies in the home areas.

The Mossi provide an example of this seasonal movement, because it takes place at the end of November, when most of the crops have been harvested, and the short but exacting agricultural period is over. Prepubescent boys or married men who have taken on the responsibilities of family life are discouraged from migrating and so the migrants are usually in the 16–30 age group. According to Skinner, the procedure is as follows (1965, p. 67):

> Those men who contemplate migration prepare for it as inconspicuously as possible so as not to arouse the attention of their relatives who would try to persuade them to remain at home. They save money and collect small livestock for sale in order to pay for their transportation. When the migrants leave, they usually slip out of their compounds 'at the first crowing of the cock' (about 3 a.m.) and take to the road where they meet with friends at prearranged places, or go on alone until they encounter other migrants along the way. Migrants travel mostly in the early

morning hours, buying breakfast from women vendors along the road before setting off. They rest during the hot part of the day and travel again in the afternoon until sundown. They customarily sleep on the outskirts of villages near clumps of trees called *kumasi kakanga*. They avoid the village centers for fear that they may be accused of theft if some villager loses his property. But they stay close to villages and away from wooded areas and rivers so as to avoid encounters with marauding beasts. They travel in this manner until the money they carry is sufficient to pay their fare to Ghana or the Ivory Coast; if they have no money, they proceed on foot or do odd jobs along the way in order to get funds to pay for transportation.

Not surprisingly, therefore, it is the most impoverished areas with poor land and no export crops which have the largest proportion of migrants absent. In Malawi, for example, Margaret Read (1942) found that 62 per cent of this group were classified as permanently absent. The wealthiest part of the country has only 24 per cent of its men away, and only 33 per cent of those were regarded as a total loss to tribal people concerned.[4]

Most Mossi migrants are prepared to take any kind of job, 'even women's work', provided they can earn money. The objective is to save as much of it as possible during the five or six months away from home; then, when there are signs of the rains starting, the migrants collect their wages and head for the markets where they buy the goods they desire. They purchase zinc buckets, kerosene lamps, long robes, cotton shirts, pants, head scarves for women, Moslem-type fezes, mirrors, sandals, mosquito nets, wooden bedsteads, eating utensils, and cement for plastering walls and floors. Although these men try to ascertain where most jobs are available before leaving home, few such migrants know exactly where they will go or what kind of work they will obtain. Others, however, do have a definite destination in view; later on, if they are disappointed in their job they will move on quickly and seek a different place, but the old hands come back each year to the same work and habits. In either case the return home of the long-distance migrant is a triumph. He is welcomed back by the head of his village and by his friends, and he gives them money and drink in return. He also distributes largesse to the minstrels who accompany him on his tour of the markets, singing his praises, while his relatives show by their new clothes and presents that they, too, have benefited from his absence (Skinner, *op. cit.*).

All this suggests that for many of the younger men migration has become virtually a modern form of initiation rite. As Rouch has remarked, they are now expected to undergo 'immersion' in an urban environment, and a youth cannot expect to win a girl's favours unless he can show the 'brand of the town upon him' (1954, pp. 19, 22).

The idea of labour migration being some kind of *rite de passage* is also found in other parts of the continent. Among the Nyakusa, for example, not only does the returned migrant gain a certain prestige from his new wealth and foreign experience, but women, unmarried and married alike, are said to be attracted by a bright shirt and shiny shoes. This was the attitude that Gulliver found in the early 1950s; and in Botswana, too, the girls preferred men who had faced the risks of town life and sent back money and presents to their relatives at home. The fact that in this way the men have shown themselves willing and able to work for the support of a family is regarded as a good augury for marriage itself. Somewhat similarly among the Alur of Uganda, not only is labour migration a way of impressing the girls, but the young men concerned use part of their earnings as a way of achieving leadership positions that were not available at home owing to age and status restrictions (Southall, 1954, p. 150).

Attitudes towards migration are important because of their effect upon the town's social organization. They raise the question, for example, of how far the migrant himself, or herself, is prepared to identify with the urban community to which he or she moves. There is no simple answer to this although it depends in part upon official policy which, during colonial times, was divided between capitalism's need of labour and the government's desire to keep the traditional agrarian system intact. In British Central Africa, for example, the main economic enterprise was mining for which Europeans were available as managers, supervisors and skilled workers, Africans only being employed as labourers. The administration of the rural areas from which they came was based upon 'tribal integrity', and this idea was also implicit in the tax census in respect of which a tribesman was *de facto* resident in the village. The consequence was that in many of the industrial centres to which the Africans moved, wage-structures were based on the assumption that families were left behind in the rural areas where they supported themselves. In other words, the African town-dweller was treated as if he were a quasi-bachelor and not encouraged to be more than a migrant (Van Velsen, 1961, *passim*).

South African policy, though more complicated, is basically somewhat similar. Much of the national economy is based upon the exploitation of the country's gold resources, and so a small proportion of Africans, such as clerks, are retained as permanent staff, but the mining industry as a whole depends on migratory labour. These workers are engaged on contract and stay on average for periods of ten to twelve months, returning home to their peasant life in rural areas between spells of work on the mines. This system is not regarded as a temporary expedient, but as a permanent feature of the organization of African labour. The policy, it is argued, reduces the African's dependence on industrialization and, by keeping him in touch with the Reserves, provides a subsistence economy on which he can fall back in the event of unemployment. An urban pass system is used to regulate the supply of labour into the towns and the government authorities have opposed the extension of married quarters on the mines themselves, thereby augmenting the proportion of migrants living as bachelors. This restriction is in line with the aim of limiting African urban settlement as far as possible to the local need of African labour in factories, industry and business establishments and as servants in European homes.

Belgian policy, however, was different. It, too, sought to regulate African migration to the towns, but in order to establish a permanent urban class of Africans. This was to consist of artisans and lower clerical workers, together with the unskilled workers required. The Belgian aim, thus, was to stabilize this labour force, first by allocating them land on which to build and, later, by providing subsidized housing to be bought by the occupants. Unlike, therefore, the African townsmen of most of South and Central Africa, the urban Congolese were not expected to be migrant workers, at least as far as the majority were concerned. Rather was it Belgian policy to keep both rural and urban populations stable. It tried to encourage the setting up of households based on the monogamous family, living permanently in town and providing a flow of both skilled and unskilled labour for the economic enterprises of the city. The Belgians also influenced the town's social composition by

15

emphasizing incipient class divisions at the expense of tribal affiliation.[5]

In British West Africa, on the other hand, there was no fixed policy. The countryside was governed through the traditional rulers, but in the coastal cities municipal affairs were largely under African control (cf. Banton, 1954, pp. 140–4) and Africans were free to come and go at will between the rural villages and the towns. This is one of the reasons why the 'lure' of city life is probably stronger in West Africa than elsewhere and is sometimes expressed in the migrants' own songs: 'Qui n'a pas été à Kumasi, n'ira pas au Paradis' is one such refrain. Doubtless it conveys very truly rustic reactions to the relative whirl and bustle of the Ashanti capital, which, by comparison with the remote villages, seems to be an El Dorado. Like London and Dublin, its streets are 'paved with gold', and so some of the younger people move townward for adventure.[6]

Cyprian Ekwensi's novels document very graphically attitudes of this kind, particularly those of the women. In one of these stories, *Jagua Nana*, a devotee of the gay life of Lagos, is deserted by her lover and falls on evil days. Returning to her own people upcountry, she is offered security and a good home by an elderly admirer, but the city's hold over her is too strong. Better, from her point of view, the squalor of a Lagos slum so long as there are sophisticated people around her, the bright lights of a night-spot, a 'highlife' band, and the chance of picking up a young well-to-do patron (Ekwensi, 1961, *passim*).

But other youths and girls younger than Ekwensi's heroine abscond and arrive eventually at the cosmopolitan towns because their home life is unhappy. Perhaps a father or a mother has remarried and the child has been left to the mercy of an unsympathetic step-parent or guardian. Motor transport makes escape comparatively easy. If a runaway finds a relative or friends to provide lodgings so much the better; if not he soon learns the trick of living by his wits and of sleeping at night within a shed at the market or in some deserted building (Busia, 1950, p. 96). So accustomed do some of these youthful vagrants become to a life of wandering that they eventually lose all sense of home ties and of their native village. Quite often the boys become members of delinquent gangs while the girls generally drift into prostitution (*ibid.*, pp. 84–105). A youth who is fortunate may arrange to apprentice himself as 'motor boy' to the driver of a lorry. His job is to help service the vehicle, look after passengers, goods, etc. In return for these services the 'motor boy' is paid a small daily wage and may be able to do a profitable trade in vehicle spare parts as well as earning tips. With the prospects of promotion to driver it is an attractive opening which draws even literate youths who have had, perhaps, a few years at school (Banton, 1957, p. 56).

More commonly, however, migration may be a way of escaping local taxes and court fees and maltreatment at the hands of an older relative or husband. In his study of Freetown, Banton (1957) interviewed migrants from the Sierra Leone provinces and they stressed not only that they could obtain finer things for their money, but that in Freetown they were free from the oppression of the chiefs and elders. In their chiefdoms they were subject to extortion if they showed too much ambition or got into trouble over women; a husband could demand as much as £12 or more for 'woman damage' and would be supported by his chiefs.[7] Similarly, in Stanleyville the village is thought of nostalgically sometimes, for the economic and social security of family life and for the abundance of food, but life in the towns was said to offer an escape from the 'harsh' authority of tribal chiefs, from sorcery, from drudgery in the fields, from obligations to demanding kinsmen and from local hostilities and jealousies of the village (Douchy and Feldheim, 1956).

Possibly the latter attitudes are explained by the planned nature, already mentioned, of African settlement in the Congolese cities. This contrasts with the more general situation, whereby the question of permanent residence is either left to chance or made very difficult. In the latter case, as indicated, Africans are induced to migrate as individual workers, but discouraged from settling with their family. When, therefore, wage-employment is virtually the only inducement, experience of urban conditions probably strengthens, rather than weakens, traditional feelings and attachments. This is suggested by the outlook of several East and Central African peoples. The Ngoni of Southern Tanzania, for example, have little or no desire to go outside their own territory or very far from their everyday community. They much prefer to remain at home and only in dire necessity do they seek work outside their own villages. In fact, following a study of this situation Gulliver reports that out of more than 2,500 journeys, some 90 per cent were made for economic reasons (1960, p. 267) and in an earlier but

17

comparable investigation made by Schapera in Bechuanaland (now Botswana) (1947) only 1·8 per cent of his sample gave non-economic reasons for their migration. The Nyakusa, too, commonly affirm that they really prefer to remain at home and live the rural life they like. Through going to the Copper Belt to earn enough money for goods – chiefly cattle – they take the job that realizes the sum needed as quickly as possible and when they have reached that target they pack up and go home. These Nyakusa migrants are struck by the high standards of living which they find and by the rich variety of goods and services so obtained with their high wages, but without feeling that those urban areas are so attractive as their own villages. They remain unimpressed by what appear to the European or urbanized African as the amenities and satisfaction of the town, and 'such things as cinemas or football conspicuously fail to attract them, even less to induce them to stay' (Gulliver, 1960, pp. 159–63).[8]

Skinner, too, tried to discover whether some of the Mossi migrants were led to travel by a desire for adventure or for amusement, and was told, 'one does not go to Kumasi to give one's money to the movies or to women'. When he pointed out that there were men who had resided in the Gold Coast for several years and who might have been seduced by city pleasures, the immediate reply was: 'Perhaps, but the hearts of such men have changed' (meaning that they have lost their heads) (Skinner, *op. cit.,* pp. 66, 67).

Among other peoples attitudes of hostility are even stronger: the town is regarded as evil and city life with abhorrence. This is the attitude, in particular, of the 'Red' section of the Xhosa people of South Africa, and it is in line with their conservative insistence on remaining typically pagan and illiterate, despite this 'Red' group's regular movement to the nearby city of East London (cf. Mayer, 1961, *passim*). Nor, in the absence of sufficient economic inducement, are migrants willing to abandon their holdings in the countryside. This objection arises because, as Elkan (1960, p. 300 and *passim*) points out, where there is no freehold type of tenure a man cannot sell his land. Nor can he even claim compensation for 'improvements', such as the house he has built or the permanent crops that he may have planted. Even if there were freehold tenure, he might not be able to sell his farm in an area where, as in most parts of Africa, land is plentiful and therefore does not command a price. Normally the sale of an asset compensates the dweller for the income which he might have expected to earn from it over the year to come. But in most parts of Africa farms cannot be sold and a man who leaves his farm simply forgoes a part of his income, for the rural income is one which cannot be compounded or capitalized. Men enjoy income from the land so long as the land is worked. There is no compensation for a permanent withdrawal from the countryside.

The upshot of all this is that migrants are often at great pains to safeguard their position at home. The Tonga – a typical example – migrate a thousand miles or more from Lake Nyasa, leaving their families behind in the care of kinsfolk or in-laws. These men work in the mines of Zambia, Rhodesia and South Africa, and a husband sends back money to his wife and also provides his relatives with financial help to pay a fine, damages or bridewealth, and to buy clothes and other necessities. In return for these and other services, the man who is away expects his kinsfolk at home to protect his membership of and his place in Tonga society. He regards his contribution of cash and goods to the rural economy as a kind of insurance premium protecting, in particular, his own rights to land.[9] Also, by letter-writing and by periodic visits home, he does what he can to keep in touch with local affairs (Van Velsen, *op. cit.*, *passim*).

Finally, although we are concerned here with movement to the towns there is also, of course, labour migration to rural employment. This category of migrants go, for example, to cocoa farms in Ghana, to rural estates in Tanzania, or to European farms in Rhodesia and South Africa. In employment of this kind the worker lives under conditions that are less different from home; but the wages being relatively low, there is again but limited incentive to remain away. On the other hand, when a man is able to move to industrial centres and towns with manufacturing plants, migration provides higher wages and sometimes a greater chance of acquiring skills and advancement; it also provides housing above the village level, and better amenities. When these inducements are on the increase there is more and more encouragement for migrants to remain for a longer period or to return for additional periods (Gulliver, 1960, pp. 159–63).

This is the other side of the picture and the one with whose positive implications for urbanization succeeding chapters will be largely concerned.

2

Modern urbanization and its opportunistic undertones

In the last chapter I laid emphasis on the rural exodus as one of the most important characteristics of social change in contemporary Africa. The result of this urban migration is that city growth there seems now to be proceeding more rapidly than in other continents. For example, Lagos had a population of 126,000 in 1930; this rose to 364,000 by 1964 and a recent estimate (1968) puts the population of Greater Lagos at 1·2 millions. On the other side of Africa, Nairobi doubled in size during the 1940–50 decade and then doubled again in the 1950–60 decade. Rates of urban growth have also been considerable in the Francophone countries. The population of the principal towns of Senegal, for example, increased by 100 per cent between 1942 and 1952; those of the Ivory Coast by 109 per cent during the same decade; and those in the Cameroons by 250 per cent between 1936 and 1952. Léopoldville (now Kinshasa) was a large country town of 34,000 in 1930, but in twenty years it had 208,000 inhabitants, a sevenfold increase. Its population was estimated in 1963 to be about a million and a quarter.[1]

Presumably, the great mass of the population of sub-Saharan Africa has always been rural. True, Arabs dealing in slaves brought some towns into being in the 'Swahili' coast of what is now Tanzania and Kenya.[2] But, as mentioned, much more significant were the powerful empires and kingdoms in the Western Sudan whose administration and commercial activities were frequently centred on settlements which were, in Louis Wirth's definition of the city, 'relatively large, dense and permanent'. For example, Abomey, the capital of Dahomey, had a population in the neighbourhood of 24,000 in 1772, and the number of Kumasi's inhabitants was estimated at between 20,000 and 25,000 in 1888 (Bascom, 1959, p. 30).

20

Also, according to Bascom's figures, not only did over 30 per cent of the some 5 million Yoruba of Western Nigeria live, in 1952, in towns of over 40,000 inhabitants, but he quotes historical evidence suggesting that urban settlement in nineteenth-century Yorubaland was equally populous and dense. For instance, Clapperton and Lander, who were the first European visitors to this region, evidently felt that the population of Ilorin, Igboho and perhaps Kishi, which still exist today, exceeded 20,000. Also, archaeological discoveries at Ife (today a city of over 130,000) indicate that it was far more important as a centre of elaborate ritual and art in earlier times; and, perhaps most remarkable of all, is Ijebu-Ode, near the coast. This is described on a Portuguese map of about 1500 as 'a very large city . . . surrounded by a moat' which may have been twenty to twenty-five feet deep and forty feet wide. The recent investigations upon which this surmise is based also discovered an enormous earth rampart, eighty miles long, enclosing an area of 400 square miles, which surrounds the existing town at distances of about five to fifteen miles (Bascom, 1963, pp. 164–85).

It would seem that structures of this kind were built for defensive purposes. The Yoruba are agriculturists whose farms are made on a wide belt of land surrounding the town, and the city itself probably arose out of the need of a rural people for a place where they could live in comparative safety while carrying on their business as farmers. Since farming was based largely on family and kinship, these institutions set the pattern of life in both city and countryside. Among the town's population there were also weavers, dyers, ironworkers, diviners and medicine men who supplied all other members of the community, including smaller towns and villages, with their particular goods and services. Nevertheless, although diversified to an extent that made each individual economically dependent on the society as a whole, such a city lacked the degree of specialization of a modern industrial economy. It served as a centre of warfare and trade, but kinship was the principal factor and primary determinant of behaviour in every aspect of community life. Moreover, during those pre-colonial times, it was within the same such city that most of its inhabitants were born and reared, married and trained their children, resided with their families throughout most of their lives, died and were buried. Ties with the lineage were not broken by urban life, nor even temporarily suspended. The authority of the family, lineage

21

and the chiefdom was maintained according to traditional standards (*ibid.*).

To some extent this traditional urbanism still holds for some of those indigenously founded West African cities which fall broadly within Southall's category of 'old established, slowly growing towns'. He distinguishes between this kind (type A) and the 'new populations of mushroom growth' (type B). Type B are exemplified by most towns in the Republic of South Africa, Zambia, Rhodesia, Kenya and Zaire, including Johannesburg, the Copper Belt, Salisbury, and Nairobi. Southall considers that most towns in Tanzania and Uganda as well as in the former territories of French Equatorial and British and French Africa belong to category A (1961, pp. 6–11). However, not only are many towns in the latter region of relatively early origin, they also retain, in several cases, very much more of their traditional character than the East African ones. Oshogbo, on the road between Lagos and Kaduna, for example, was founded about 1880. When reported on by Schwab in 1965 it had more than 120,000 inhabitants whose livelihood continued to depend mainly on agriculture. Farmland extended for as little as two miles to as much as ten miles on all sides of the town. Despite immigration into it, Oshogbo still had a stable, ethnically homogeneous population sharing a fundamentally unitary system of values. There was a number of well-to-do traders and some clerks and teachers, but economic standards were substantially uniform. Also, although sentiments of common descent have been somewhat weakened by new interests and values, the corporate solidarity of the lineage had not been destroyed. Consequently, and because persons were still compelled to conform to traditional norms and behaviour defined primarily by kinship, no sharply differentiated social class system had developed (Schwab, 1965, pp. 85–109).

In fact, therefore, although relative age and rate of growth may sometimes be useful criteria for distinguishing between African towns, the more relevant question is whether they are *sociologically* 'traditional' or 'modern'. Kumasi, as explained, has probably existed for several centuries, but its conversion into a flourishing centre of commerce and communications is more significant for contemporary urban type than Kumasi's antiquity. Oshogbo, again, has roughly doubled in size during the decade 1952–62 and Accra has grown at approximately the same rate. However, the influx into the former town seems to have been mainly in terms of the same Yoruba ethnic group as Oshogbo's own inhabitants, whereas Accra contains more than eighty different peoples and tribes and only about one half of its population are indigenous to that area. Further, although Kampala goes back to the late nineteenth century, it was estimated fairly recently that those who had lived continuously there for five years or more accounted for less than 20 per cent of the population (Gutkind, 1962).[3]

Impermanence of residence, therefore, is an important mark of urban character in what we choose to call the 'modern' town. A large proportion of its inhabitants are transitory because, as explained, much of the immigration upon which the population is based is seasonal and 'circular'. In other words, as described in several places elsewhere, the workers concerned tend to come and go and do not necessarily return each time to the same town. In this case, when, as in the many recently established towns and urban agglomerations, the majority of inhabitants are newcomers, the stress laid by Southall on 'mushroom' growth involves no ambiguity. For instance, according to Balandier's study (1955, p. 148) less than 10 per cent of the population of Poto Poto (one of the three African townships of Brazzaville) were born in that city; and Enugu, founded in 1914 on an empty site, had some 82,000 inhabitants by 1962.

Needless to say, cultural heterogeneity is also increased by the presence of Asians, including Indians, Pakistanis, Arabs and Lebanese. There are in addition Europeans and other non-African 'expatriates' and about all these groups more will be said in the context of race relations. The fact, however, that Europeans are largely in supervisory and managerial occupations and the Asians in commerce is relevant here as being symptomatic of a general tendency towards ethnic and tribal specialization. As will be explained in Chapter 5 the mixed population of Jinja (Uganda) is a typical case in this regard.

In Accra, occupational specialization among the African population *per se* involves the majority of fishermen and farmers being Ga and Adangme; most of the semi-skilled and skilled workers for the manufacturing industry being supplied by tribes in southern Ghana and Ashanti; and the educated workers in clerical, executive and administrative posts being provided by southern Ghana (Little, 1965, p. 4).

23

c

It goes without saying, in other words, that in the 'modern' town a relatively large proportion of the inhabitants are involved in a monetary economy. The extent, as we shall attempt to show, varies obviously with industrialization and similar forces. However, a final important factor, noted by several authors, is demographic rather than economic.[4] This is the numerical preponderance of young people over old, and to a less appreciable extent the preponderance of adult males over women. Generally, too, the more remote the migrants' rural home from their urban place of temporary settlement, the greater the proportion of men, with the result that, in these groups, male migrants may be six or seven times more numerous than females.[5]

The above characteristics of the 'modern' town result from its being mostly a product of forces external not only to itself but to African society in general. Having developed mainly in response to commercial and industrial demands from overseas, its existence serves a variety of functions emanating from a marketing economy whose origin is international rather than local or even national.[6] It is through the effect of this situation that the 'modern' town contrasts so sharply with the kind of *rus in urbe* described above. Whereas, in the latter case, social life is organized on a basis of kinship and local community, in contemporary cities and industrial centres like Accra and Lagos, Nairobi, Kinshasa, Dar es Salaam and the Zambian Copper Belt, the basis of a person's livelihood is different. It tends to depend not on membership of the extended family but on the sale of labour, goods and personal services. This means that, although there are variations not only between particular towns but between sections of the same town's population, a communalistic pattern of behaviour has been largely replaced by an individualistic one. It means that the 'modern' town is geared largely to the demands of exogenous economic forces, it operates as part of a superimposed, urban-industrial system (see Chapter 7). Consequently, status and position are very much more a matter of achievement than in rural peasant society.

It follows that this new assignment of roles is primarily to individuals who possess western education and training. An African social category of this kind came embryonically into being during earlier European contact and throughout the period of the Slave Trade, when it took the form of small westernized communities living close to the forts and barracoons of the West Coast

24

(Wyndham, 1935). Both there and elsewhere this category of African served as clerks, interpreters and intermediaries between the local African rulers and the European traders and merchants. Later, the Sierra Leone peninsula was established as a philanthropic settlement for Negroes from Britain, Nova Scotia and Jamaica, and Freetown became the principal port from which British efforts to stamp out the Slave Trade were made. Africans recaptured from the slavers were landed there and placed under the care of churchmen and missionaries who, in addition to evangelizing, provided their charges with schools. As a result, this Creole population (as it was later called) became the most highly educated group of Africans in the whole sub-continent.[7] Numbers of them thrived commercially and became wealthy enough to send their children to Britain for training. Individual Creoles were also members of the colonial legislature and since there was a demand for literate Africans accustomed to western ways, Creoles found ready employment in government departments and trading agencies in the other colonies as well as at home. In consequence, either through migration or in the ordinary course of business, these people spread out widely over the whole West African littoral. All the way from the Congo in the south to the Gambia in the west they constituted, in many cases, little oases of westernized culture. They and the local families with whom and into whom they married played a major part culturally, professionally and commercially during the earlier stages of urban development (Little, 1950, pp. 308–19). In the Francophone colonies, mainly Senegal, *évolués* had a somewhat similar role. These were Africans who had attained a relatively high standard of education, followed French customs and to whom, in certain 'communes' – for example, Dakar, Gorée, Saint Louis and Rufisque – French citizenship was accorded, including the right to elect deputies to the Chamber in Paris (see *inter alios* Mumford, 1936; O'Brien, 1972).

In the Cape Colony, members of the Coloured group were also educated to a relatively high level, and following the expansion of colonial rule more and more mission schools came into existence throughout the continent. Overall, however, for the great mass of the sub-Saharan indigenous population there were very few opportunities of taking part in modern institutions except in a subordinate capacity. With the exception of the communities mentioned, in the countries under European government the

Africans were either educationally too backward or prevented by the presence of white settlers and/or official policy, as in South Africa, from advancing occupationally to higher positions.

True, especially in the West Coast, concomitant with the development of urban centres, Africans had increased chances of jobs requiring education and skill, which were also better paid. This occupational upgrading of Africans was due to the British adoption, following the First World War, of 'trusteeship' as colonial policy and, as explained in Chapter 5, it was also backed by the gathering forces of African nationalism. What, however, speeded the whole process and finally brought matters to a head was the advent of the Second World War and the events following it. The Allied war effort demanded greatly increased supplies of palm kernels, cotton, cocoa, and other locally produced raw materials, including minerals. Since the colonial governments were required to stimulate these (Fortes, 1945, pp. 205–19), the effect, in terms of strong economic and other tendencies towards social change, was felt during the 1940s all over Africa. Of the then Gold Coast, for example, Fortes reported that, to some extent, 'labour, enterprise and skill are now marketable in their own right anywhere in the country'. The general atmosphere was generative of mobility, and so moving around in modern conditions in Ashanti was 'a response to the present instability of all social norms which springs in part from the cocoa trade and its resultants, in particular, the advent of a money economy' (1947, pp. 164–5).

Agitation for African self-government gave a more specific meaning to this restlessness; and, consequent, in particular, upon the tremendous economic boom following the Second World War[8] as well as upon Independence itself, changes in the whole structure of African society took place at an even greater pace than before.[9] This happened largely because of the much increased number of high-ranking places in the civil service, business, and in other sectors of the economy that economic expansion created and Independence made available to Africans. Of course, throughout the colonial era, African chiefs and other traditional rulers usually had local charge, under varying degrees of supervision, of the rural areas. But, as explained, at the national level most of the few positions of authority and influence to which, previously, Africans might aspire were filled by the *évolués* and by members of the westernized intelligentsia. Now, there were plenty of vacancies, and with more jobs going than there were adequately qualified Africans to fill, the educational system was broadened and the production of university graduates stepped up.

In fact, prior to 1948, only one institution of higher learning existed in the whole of 'black' Africa. This was the Fourah Bay College in Freetown which had functioned from 1876 as one of Durham University's colleges. In 1948, however, university colleges were founded at Ibadan, Nigeria and at Legon, near Accra, and these became full universities in the early 1960s. In Uganda, Makerere was made a university college in 1949, and a university college for Rhodesia and Nyasaland was founded in 1955. Nyasaland (now Malawi) did not have its own university until 1964, nor Zambia until 1965, but university colleges in both Kenya and Tanzania had been opened a few years earlier. In Francophone Africa, however, facilities for higher education are still more meagre and even Dakar did not have a university at all until 1957. This was a year after Lovanium – previously known as the Congolese University Centre – was given the full title of university. In the adjoining Congo Republic (Brazzaville) a 'university agency' was created in 1961 and in the Ivory Coast the *Centre d'Enseignement Supérieur* achieved status as the University of Abidjan in 1963 (Sasnett and Sempeyer, 1966; and Association of Commonwealth Universities, 1971).

'Africanization' and kindred developments are exemplified most strikingly by the Western Region of Nigeria where free primary education was provided in 1958 for all children of school age and the number of grammar schools quadrupled in a decade. In respect of the professions and the civil service, in the early 1950s there was a large proportion of Nigerians in education, medicine and law, but almost none in the administrative service. In the latter's ranks there was but one Nigerian, and even in 1956 two-thirds of the men in 'A' scale and super-scale posts were expatriates. A few Nigerians were appointed to junior posts in 1954 and in the following year the intake of Nigerian university graduates really began. Its speed and effect was such that Lloyd was able to report in 1967 that 'Today, there are about 650 Nigerians in super-scale posts against about 150 expatriates'. Naturally, the civil service itself had expanded, there being a rise of 25 per cent between 1957–63 in the administrative and professional and super-scale posts, and a threefold increase in the executive and technical grades. Somewhat similarly, in Ghana prior to Independence, professional people numbered only a few hundred, including 57 judges, barristers or solicitors and 45 doctors and dentists. By 1954 the proportion of Africans in senior posts rose from 13·8 per cent in 1949 to 38·2 per cent (Lloyd, 1967, pp. 129–50).[10] In Nigeria, all permanent secretaries being now Nigerian has meant rapid promotion within the upper grades and particularly for those graduates who joined the civil service in the 1950s. It has been even faster in the administrative branches as the establishment increased, the (European) 'expatriates' left, and a series of new ranks was created. In the public corporations, conditions of employment and salary structure being very similar to those of the regional civil service, patterns of rapid expansion, rapid Nigerianization, and rapid promotion were repeated. In, for example, the University of Ibadan, one-third of the senior staff are Nigerians, and promotion from the lecturer grade (£1,200 per annum) to a professorship (£3,000 per annum) within six or seven years has become a common practice (*ibid.*).

In fact, so rapidly did men in Ibadan improve their position that, according to Lloyd, 'within twenty years of their own lifetimes many have moved from a traditional compound . . . of a poor farmer to a modern government or university house furnished in a manner appropriate to a four figure salary'. This can be seen very clearly in home backgrounds. For example, two-fifths of those with post-secondary education had fathers who never attended school and who were, in consequence, farmers or poorly-off craftsmen. Between two-thirds and three-quarters had illiterate mothers and only one-quarter had fathers who received post-primary education. These latter fathers – the élite of their own generation – were chief clerks, primary school headmasters, clergymen and so on; and the social characteristics of Ibadan university students have continued to tell a somewhat similar story. True, in their case the proportion of fathers belonging to what Lloyd calls the 'modern élite' and 'sub-élite' rose to 40 per cent; but one-third of the fathers belonged to farming families and about 36 per cent of the mothers were in trading (Van den Berghe, 1969, pp. 355–78).[11] Further, although about one-third of the Nigerians are from professional or semi-professional homes, only about one-tenth of Kenyan, Tanzanian and Ugandan students have this kind of origin (*ibid.*) while students at the University of Ghana, too, were found to be drawn from the lower middle class of clerks, small traders, and minor professionals. Unlike their predecessors, these students had, as a rule, little or no background of western tradition, because only a small proportion of the parents had been to school. Out of 476 pairs of grandparents, nearly 70 per cent were totally illiterate, and the illiteracy rate of both parents was 75 per cent. Even among a sample of Ghanaian senior civil servants, about one out of every three was found to have an illiterate father (Jahoda, 1955; Peil, 1965; Oppong, 1974).

These much increased opportunities of higher education naturally meant that, instead of the 'old' families the influential and well-to-do class now consisted largely of 'new' men. The effect of this was to generate feelings of optimism and even euphoria. Since, in theory at least, there was nothing to prevent an office messenger rising to be a permanent secretary, able, energetic and educated young men might very well feel that they carried, so to speak, a ministerial portfolio within their briefcase. Admittedly, it was a far cry from the mud hut to the opulence of such an office,[12] but had not the beginning of several of Africa's most celebrated heads of State been equally humble? Kwame Nkrumah's own family, for example, was locally of little importance and belonged to one of the smaller and less well-known tribes of the then Gold Coast. Dr Hastings Banda, President of Malawi, started his career as a labour migrant, working as a clerk at a Witwatersrand mine; and, before he became a political leader and gained the presidential office in Zambia, Dr Kenneth Kaunda taught in a small mission school. Other men in high positions were born in the same village as those who now sought to emulate their career, and since such successful politicians had risen to the top without apparent difficulty, it was evidently necessary merely to play one's cards skilfully and to cultivate the right people. As the narrator in Achebe's characterization of an *arriviste* Federal Minister remarks: 'A common saying ... after Independence was that it didn't matter *what* you knew but *who* you knew. And, believe me, it was no idle talk' (1966, p. 19).

Since this kind of attitude placed, quite obviously, a special premium on opportunism, opportunistic patterns of behaviour naturally developed. This was the case especially in politics, the example *par excellence* being undoubtedly the former Congo. There, Belgian policy had restricted the role of educated Africans to that of *petite bourgeoisie;* and so, when the colonialists' sudden exodus placed within African reach the immediate prize of political power, the Congolese élite essaying to grasp it possessed no experience at all of the realities of such responsibility. This simply meant, when the Belgians had gone, that individual politicians jockeyed for position and that political groupings were mobilized for particular purposes but did not constitute permanent corporate groupings. Nor, with one doubtful exception, was any party concerned with either a political ideology or a government plan. Even the Prime Minister himself was not a member of a party; his was a government of individuals (La Fontaine, 1970, pp. 191ff.).

According to some observers, opportunism in a more general sense was also characteristically exhibited by student behaviour in relation to prospective careers. For example, after studying the attitude of a sample of Ghanaians, Margaret Peil wrote (1965, pp. 19–28) that many of them:

> simply do not consider arriving at a specific job; they will take whatever opportunities are presented. A student may be very enthusiastic about something, and convince you that this is his goal in life; three months later you may find him in a different job, having seemingly forgotten all about his previous enthusiasm. All this makes for flexibility, but one wonders if it makes for long term dedication. If the current job represents only what is opportune at the moment, and will be dropped when a better one is in sight, why put oneself out?

A similar note, combined with optimism, was struck by a group of Ghanaian male and female students whom Jahoda studied. He asked them to name the kind of job they anticipated entering immediately after leaving college and what were their long-term aims; what would they like to be doing in twenty years time? Results showed that most of the students expected to get to the top, or at least near the top, of their chosen profession. Many regarded teaching or the civil service *merely as springboards* (my italics) for the realization of other ambitions, although 40 per cent of Arts and 63 per cent of Science students intended to remain within the same broad occupational group. Some of the more glamorous-appearing callings accounted for one-fifth of Arts students' ultimate choices, e.g. authorship, politics, diplomacy and so on. ('I want to be an ambassador of Ghana to a foreign country.') About another fifth seemed to be primarily concerned with the material rewards of the job but approximately one-quarter proposed to remain within the educational field – of course usually at a fairly high level. Among the remainder, the traditionally high-prestige occupations of lawyer and civil service (at the permanent secretary level) were most important (Jahoda, 1955).

In more general terms, too, the opportunism referred to above seems to be reflected in the readiness of people to change their employment. As Fortes had already noted in the 1940s people moved about the more readily if their learning capacity was low, but this tendency is also strong among literate people as well as among men lacking education and technical skills. Thus, a boy may go into teaching or do a bit of farming, or become a levy-collector for a short period until he finds something better. Even long-held occupations are not considered permanent. After several years of teaching a man may farm cocoa for a season or become a lawyer. A man who has farmed for twenty years may decide to take up carpentry, etc. A rather extreme case, quoted by Peil, was a man applying for a lower administrative position who had already been a veterinary assistant, a railway stationmaster, and a student of Chinese linguistics (Peil, 1968, *passim*).

In short, it would appear that the urban situation which has emerged involves not only the appearance of entirely new structures but can, perhaps, be characterized with some validity, as an 'opportunistic society'.[13] The further implications of this kind of social environment for attitudes to work and to wage-employment, in particular, will be briefly considered in the next chapter.

3

Attitudes to work and wage-employment

In the last chapter, having mentioned the transient behaviour of many urban inhabitants, we described the growth of opportunism and coupled it with occupational mobility. It is necessary to elaborate on these factors because they not only contribute to the impermanent character of the modern town's population, but help to explain it. Thus, in a further case cited by Peil (1972, pp. 55–9), a Hausa from Niger came to Ghana at about 20 years of age and worked as a *kayakaya* (porter) for 5 years, then as a stone-cracker for 2 years, a miner for 6 years and a soldier for 7 years, before he returned home in the late 1940s for 2 years' farming. Each of his Ghanaian jobs took him to a new place. He returned to Ghana and did contracting for 2 years. Then he worked as a watchman for the government for 2 years before moving back to Accra in 1952. In this case there was no commitment to any particular job. He merely took whatever came along and left when he tired of it. In addition, Peil found a Ga supervisor of 68 who grew up in Accra and has only lived elsewhere for three years. He started working at 21 as a beach clerk, then moved to Nswawam (twenty miles from Accra) as a buyer of foodstuffs on his own account. Returning to Accra in 1921 he worked for 6 years as a customs clerk, then farmed for 5 years, spent 3 years in the army in the early 1930s and went back to farming for about 17 years. He left this in 1954 to become a customs clerk and later supervisor for his Lebanese employer.

Such mobility is encouraged because the relatively low requirements of most jobs mean that workers can easily move from one occupation to another. But where opportunism prevails, there appears to be relatively little resistance to the idea of something completely new at any stage of one's career, even if it has involved extensive preparation. 'This attitude', remarks Peil, 'seems ideal for a rapidly changing society, but it does mean that a good deal of training is wasted when the recipient moves on to something completely different.' The result is that many workers in their fifties and sixties have had a very mixed career,[1] and although skilled workers more often stick to one occupation the difficulties of maintaining a satisfactory standard of living in self-employment have forced many of them to pick up new skills and seek wage-employment. The fact that many of the young men are willing to leave home and risk unemployment or endure its effects for extended periods is due to their desire for cash earnings. The income gained is low in comparison with the wages paid in developed countries and may not be much higher than what is needed to supply the essentials of urban life. Nevertheless, they often represent the opportunity of improving one's standard of living considerably beyond the village level. In the traditional system governing rural life young men have little standing, so that urban wages represent a chance for independence.

However, despite the evidence of transience adduced, there are signs also that migrants coming to town stay longer on each occasion. These men, as Plotnicov has shown from his Jos (Northern Nigeria) study (1967, pp. 283–5), are increasingly reluctant to maintain close rural ties and even more reluctant to retire to the rural areas. Migrant labour may set up a chain-reaction in this regard as when, in Central Africa for example, it became more and more institutionalized as the rural areas' principal mode of involvement in the money economy. In other words, interaction between village and town correspondingly increased and migrants stayed for ever longer periods in the industrial centres. The result was that, by 1951, two-fifths of the men on the Copper Belt, for example, had lived ten years or more in urban areas and about the same proportion had wives living with them. Previously, all three agencies – the government, the mining companies and the tribal authorities – had restricted in various ways the movement of women to the towns (Heisler, 1971). In terms of money values, urban incomes were two and a half times as large in Zambia as estimated *per capita* peasant incomes in 1954, three and a half times greater in 1964, but seven times greater in 1960 (*ibid.*).

On the other hand, it also happens that migrants taking urban jobs may be worse off than at home because they must now pay for goods which they or their wives provided in the village for family use (Boserup, 1970, pp. 170–2). There is also a good deal of urban unemployment with the result, according to some sample surveys, that quite a considerable proportion of the male population of most African towns is out of work (Gutkind, 1968).[2] One such place is the Federal Territory of Lagos where, in an estimated population of 600,000, some 65,000 persons, all males, were said in 1964 to be actively seeking employment (*ibid.*).

If, therefore, we are thinking of the work situation alone, African responses to the changing economic order have been varied. They range from a total commitment, as among miners, dock workers, and the more skilled factory and commercial workers, to the partial commitment of migrant and casual workers. But provided that the migrant type of labour appears as the most economic choice for the African, the social and economic role played by such labour is likely to continue for some time to come. For this reason it is all the more important to understand attitudes to work itself, because when such men board the lorries they are embarking on a journey which takes them not merely to another district but to a different belief system. They leave societies organized on a kinship basis which give them rights and obligations as members of a family and in which there is no place for economic individualism. Yet, it is this which dominates the environment they have to work in, and means they are setting, so to speak, one foot in the industrial system while the other remains in rural society. That their commitment to the former is only temporary colours their attitude towards the jobs they undertake, hence the readiness with which they transfer from one situation to another is, in turn, strengthened by the labour market's own fluidity, as well as by the alien nature of industrial employment.

The latter situation is alien because an employee works a given number of hours, is paid for his services an agreed sum of money, and there the contract ends. On the rural farm, by contrast, the worker may be remunerated either in money or in kind, but completion of the job does not necessarily terminate what, in industrial terminology, is referred to as the employer-employee relationship. On the contrary, by 'employing' a fellow villager the employer enters into a comprehensive and continuous relationship which may extend to protection and succour should the 'employee' subsequently have need of his help. In addition, although a man will

34

voluntarily answer the call when a fellow villager requires extra labour, the work he does is mutually regarded simply as a 'good turn' which the neighbour rendering it provides at his own convenience. Urban industrial norms, on the other hand, not only make the whole matter impersonal but enjoin punctuality, and a daily routine of regular hours to which the man from the countryside is not accustomed and which he finds unduly monotonous (Charles, 1952; see also Wober, 1967, pp. 183–92, and 1971, pp. 67–78).

In these regards, too, a related consideration emerges from Wober's study of attitudes towards work in Sapele's (Nigeria) timber industry. He found that levels of satisfaction may be relative to how the status of the self stands with regard to workers' relevant reference groups. Thus, there appeared to be least satisfaction among the unskilled workers and this was possibly because the difference between peasant and unskilled worker may be smaller, subjectively speaking, than between clerk and intelligentsia. This meant that it may do little for the least skilled man to feel better placed than a peasant if his job satisfaction is low, while the clerk, being less worried by a distinction between himself and the 'intellectuals', feel more satisfied by his work. On the other hand, clerks, apparently, get on less well than do manual workers with their supervisors and this may be on account of 'frustration'. Clerks, in other words, identify themselves with their supervisors' status without being realistically in a position to achieve it. Wober found that what both clerks and manual workers liked about the firm employing them was its provision of free medical treatment and of scholarships for training some sons of workers. The regularity of pay was also appreciated and the workers seemed to take some pride in belonging to an up-to-date, efficient industry. Also, consonant with the point made above about rural values, several men apparently felt that the company existed for the betterment of its employees. In other words, they accorded to it a paternal, protective role, implying that their employers may have taken over, unwittingly, some of the tribe's or the clan's traditional functions (Wober, 1971, pp. 67–78).

These considerations naturally take us, in turn, to the position of the employer. His problem is how to reduce labour turnover and how to improve the efficiency of his labour force. Workers do not reach their maximum efficiency until they have done a job for some time and to some extent the problem of how to improve efficiency resolves itself into one of getting people to stay longer in one job.

This is a point on which light has been thrown by Elkan's study of a tobacco factory in Kampala. He discovered that a very high proportion of the workers who left did so in their first year and that the background from which a man came was an important factor. For example, although workers from the local Ganda ethnic group constituted only one-eighth of those workers who had completed less than a year's service, one-third of those left were Ganda. At the same time, while the Ganda formed only 26 per cent of all employees, 54 per cent of men with three or more years' service and 53 per cent of those whose service was at least five years were Ganda. One reason, apparently, was that the Ganda had generally received more schooling than other immigrants. This gave them a slightly better chance of rising in the pay scale during the first two years, and a Ganda would stay if he saw before him a prospect of rapid increase in his earnings. In other words, the firm's policy was more successful in retaining its Ganda workers than in retaining others, and a contributory factor was that many of the Ganda possessed a small customary holding of land for which they paid a nominal rent. Since they could grow on this at least part of the food they ate, their cost of living was generally lower than that of others; and so, being materially better off, they were also able to afford and benefit from membership of a provident fund to which the firm contributed on a fifty-fifty basis (Elkan, 1956, *passim*).

Other immigrant factory workers were less satisfied, Elkan found, because, *inter alia*, they had no means of growing food and had generally overlooked the fact that wages had to cover its cost. From their point of view food was not something which one bought, and 'to eat one's wages' seemed preposterous. This attitude towards food had, in turn, an important bearing on efficiency. Since the men resented having to pay cash for food they may sometimes have spent less than was necessary to maintain health and strength. In consequence, these men were lethargic and were unable to summon the energy to work hard consistently or to make the occasional extra effort required to prevent some mishap or to do a job thoroughly. Other workers simply left. They came to Kampala to earn cash, but were unwilling to accept poor food in order to save (*ibid.*).

In fact, it was the desire to save which differentiated between attitudes towards wage-employment. The Ruanda in Kampala, for example, would live in houses which a Ganda would not tolerate and would eat the minimum consistent with staving off hunger. This was not because the Ruanda knew no better, but because they would not squander in Kampala the precious means to a better life in their own country. In contrast were those migrants who had settled in Kampala and had accepted the idea of remaining wage-earners for a large part of their lives. For them, what was urgent was not the need to save but the pressure to spend. Thus, Elkan found that of 166 Ganda employed in the factory studied, 104 drew the regular mid-monthly advance allowed by the employers. Although this meant that 63 per cent of Ganda workers took an advance compared with 44 per cent of the total labour force, it does not necessarily signify that the Ganda had more licentious habits. It merely implied that wage-employment had ceased, for the Ganda, to be the very temporary expedient which it was for the other tribes. It had become Ganda's normal habit (*ibid.*).

Finally, the position of women as workers in the urban-industrial system is to be considered, although their proportion in any sub-Saharan country probably does not amount to more than 10 per cent of the entire labour force. Nevertheless, women's relation to wage-employment is by no means unimportant because it is affected not only by the relative lag in female education but also by objections towards women earning money and to their working outside the home. For example, Elkan was told by his male informants employed in the tobacco factory at Jinja that women who went out to work would not bear children – a complaint that was particularly strong when the employment of wives involved their being under the authority of a man who was not their husband. In fact, the men's objection was not only to their own wives working for wages, but extended to any employer who was prepared to employ women (*ibid.*, pp. 45–6; see also Little, 1973a, ch. 3). Nor is this attitude confined to illiterate and semi-literate men living in a traditional way. Numbers of educated husbands, too, forbid their wives to accept posts in teaching and nursing and are equally averse to their undertaking jobs which necessitate their regular absence from the home. Indeed, male approval of women engaging in paid employment is so far from being universal that there are occasions when even an educated husband will do everything in his power to get his wife dismissed from her job (Little, 1973a, p. 181 n.).

The main reason for this negativism is the view, held by the men concerned, that for a wife to earn money not only constitutes a threat to a husband's authority and to his ability to control her, but may enable her to abscond.[3] Nor is it just the male sex who hold such 'old-fashioned' ideas of the women's role. In Kampala, Mandeville studied a large number of families living very close to and even below the 'poverty line' and found that, despite their near-destitution, many of the wives themselves ruled out certain jobs as quite unsuitable for women. These included beer-selling, spirit-selling, trading in the market, dancing professionally and working in bars. Food-selling, for example, was represented as the work of old, 'local' women, smoking and shouting obscenities; it was by no means regarded as a 'civilized' thing to do. Trading by married women also was rejected because it would bring them and their children into constant contact with strangers and undesirable company. In fact, beer brewers and dancers were in a position to make a lot of money, but these women chose poverty and 'independence' (as they saw it) in preference to jobs that were looked upon as unsuitable and degrading (Mandeville, n.d.). More-over, although Ghanaian women, in particular, have a long tradi-tion of working to support themselves, there is also a good deal of conservatism among them. Thus, Peil found that even in the relatively industrialized towns of that country female employment in factories was mostly confined to the younger women, because the working of regular hours was regarded as out of keeping with marriage and the rearing of children (1972, *passim*). On the other hand, Peil also noticed that for a given amount of education women have higher aspirations than men (*ibid.*, p. 112).

Not only, therefore, is there some incompatibility between the attitudes of workers in general and the values implicit in Western notions of industrialism, but differences in the attitudes of male and female workers as well. The former is a particularly significant consideration in the assessment of African urbanization because the assimilation of western ideals and norms as distinct from following merely conventional etiquette and customs varies with the particu-lar group. This has been shown strikingly by Mayer's comparison of the 'Red' and 'School' migrants in East London where, as he points out, even prolonged residence in the atmosphere of the city does not automatically transform country-bred people into real townsmen and townswomen. 'Red' migrants' leisure-time activities, for instance, take a traditional form, whereas the 'School' people belong to churches, athletic and social clubs, etc. (Mayer, 1961, *passim*).

Consequently, although African workers use machines, are sometimes highly skilled, and are well attuned to industrial life,[4] it does not always follow that their motivations and outlook on jobs are the same as those of European and North American factory and mine workers. In other words, what the above data seem to show is that traditional attitudes and values often carry over. They tend to influence not only the relationships of Africans with each other but their attitudes within the context of urban-industrial employment as well.

I shall endeavour to show, in succeeding chapters, the effects of this interplay of old and new values, aims, and incentives on the 'modern' African town's social structure.

D

4

Social class and ethnicity

In Ghana, the time spent in continuous employment seems to have decreased, and redundancy to have increased in recent years. This is partly due to unstable economic conditions. Workers are laid off for weeks, months, or permanently because the money for development runs out, import licences are subject to long delays, import quotas are cut, or increases in the cost of living cut people's ability to buy locally-produced consumer goods. Those who grew up in villages, especially northerners and non-Ghanaians, are more likely to escape long periods of unemployment than are southerners and those of urban origin. The reason is the willingness of the former category to do unskilled work and farm, whereas the latter are oriented towards 'school leaver' jobs which take longer to find (Peil, 1972, *passim*).

Difficulties of this kind, coupled with the scarcity of housing and its high cost, probably account for a further characteristic of the 'modern' town, known as peri-urbanism. This particular phenomenon is found on the fringe of many rapidly growing cities and industrial centres, and in Blantyre (Malawi) it involves about one-third of the local labour force commuting daily from village to town. Some 62 per cent of these people reside within walking distance of it, i.e. within four miles of the built-up area, and this enables a small plot of ground to be cultivated, while one or more members of the household work, at the same time, in town for money. This combination of village horticulture and wage-employment thus provides some room for manoeuvre in the event of unemployment or there being a lack of dignified kinds of jobs (Bettison, 1961, pp. 275–80).

The implication of this ecological situation is that the modern sector of the economy expands and contracts and is, in any case, small in extent. It is true that relative to the rural countryside the incidence of wage-employment is high, but in comparison with the western city most African towns are only semi-industrialized. The tendency, moreover, is for the state's principal resources to be concentrated within one or two so-called primate cities. For example, not only does about 25 per cent of the urban population of Ghana live in Accra (Capital District), but it contains 34 per cent of persons who have attended institutions of further education. The percentage of the latter is equalled by that of electricians, although technicians, mechanics and car drivers are relatively few in number. Also, since there is a particular concentration of most of the institutions which can be found in smaller pockets of modern economic activity in the Capital District, it also has 52 per cent of the directors and managers and 58 per cent of the bookkeepers in the country as a whole. These human resources reflect the role of Accra as the seat of government and the main centre of commercial, cultural and social life of the country. In respect of capital resources, Accra alone has one-third of the total stock, including many buildings and constructions; and almost half of the value of construction in Ghana can be allocated to the Capital District. Its share, which excludes rural implements, aircraft, ships and vehicles, is about 44 per cent (UNECA, 1962, pp. 17–18).

However, even in Accra's Municipal District the proportion of men and women in professional, executive, technical, administrative and managerial occupations is only about 7·7 per cent of the total employed population, while in Kumasi – Ghana's second city – it is only about 6·2 per cent. Since it is this group who mainly operate the modern sector of the town's economy and direct and provide its principal social services, these senior civil servants, owners and managers of business concerns, doctors and lawyers, and other professionals are generally well enough off. But, between this tiny section and the great mass of the urban population, differences in income are usually considerable and, not infrequently, extreme. In Accra, for example, not only are the civil servants paid at a rate between £700 and £2,500 per year compared to average earnings of £200 per annum, but they have a number of special perquisites and allowances. These include free medical care for man, wife and children, car loans, access to subsidized, partly furnished accommodation with garden, piped water and electricity, as well as pensions on retirement. In other words, unlike the ordinary family, senior civil servants can afford the amenities of modern urban life, such as refrigerators, television sets, imported food and clothing. Moreover, not only are the salaries of this élite group four or more times higher than the average, but the gap between high and low incomes is not decreasing (Oppong, 1974). Again, in Blantyre, senior civil servants are paid nearly £3,000 per annum and managerial staff about £1,500 per annum, while for machinists in footwear and clothing factories and labourers in tobacco factories the range is respectively from £100 per annum and £150 per annum. Workers in printing and publishing earn on the average about £250 per annum, and teachers and middle-grade clerks about £300 per annum (National Statistical Office, Malawi, 1967 and 1969). In Lagos, among a sample of householders in 1959 the medium monthly income of traders and business men, clerks, self-employed skilled manual workers and labourers were respectively £20, £18, £15, £14 10s. 0d. and £7. Professionals and civil servants together constituted rather less than 10 per cent of the population and had an average income of £472 (cf. UNECA, 1962, pp. 42–3).

In Lagos, earnings probably compare favourably rather than otherwise with other large towns, such as Kampala where many people appear to fall beneath what in Europe would be called the 'poverty-line'. Thus, in the Kampala study cited above, Mandeville classified the hypothetical needs of a family of man and wife and two children in terms of diets, A, B, C and D. Diet A came first in terms of quantity, quality and cost of food and was followed in turn by diets B, C and D. Most of the men concerned were manual workers and Mandeville found, in a sample of 84 households, that 40 per cent could afford diet A and have more than 20/- a month over, 29 per cent could afford diets A, B or C with not more than 20/- over, 13 per cent could afford D, and 18 per cent could not afford even D. She also discovered that difference in income, and not the presence of children, was responsible for the inability to afford a better diet. In a further sample of 27 households, 33 per cent could afford diet A with more than 20/- a month to spare, 33 per cent could afford A with less, or B or C, 19 per cent could afford D, and 15 per cent could not afford even D. More than half of these households paid no rent, and for most of those who did pay, rents were low. Again, the generally lower standard of living and the different distribution among households were due not to the presence of children or to payment of rents but to lower incomes. Thus, 18 per cent of the one sample and 15 per cent of the other sample could not afford to live at what seemed to be the lowest possible standard (Mandeville, n.d.).

Probably the above circumstances are by no means atypical and so, average spending power being so low, very few families can afford any modern amenities at all. This means, taking housing alone, that the majority of urban people live in rented rooms or occupy even more makeshift accommodation, often consisting of mere shacks and made out of wooden boards, corrugated iron and sheets of cardboard (cf. Marris, 1961, p. 71; UNECA, *op. cit.*). Also, overcrowding is often extreme and in a survey of Accra, for instance, 74 per cent of the households sampled by Acquah had only one room each, and a further 8 per cent were households each with under one room. Similarly, among clerks, artisans and labourers in Lagos and Enugu, some 79 per cent of 540 households in Lagos and 78·5 per cent of 389 households in Enugu were living in one-roomed homes (Federal Department of Statistics, Nigeria, 1957). Well-to-do families, on the other hand, have modern houses furnished in western style and equipped with electricity and other up-to-date appliances. Most of them use one or more motor cars and sometimes employ a chauffeur. Other servants are kept to cook, mind the children, clean the house, and wait at table. For meals it is customary to follow a standard diet of indigenous foods, but various western dishes are added. Coffee or tea is frequently served, and alcoholic beverages, particularly beer and whisky, are invariably offered to guests. These 'upper class' people are also very well provided with clothes, generally possessing several complete out-fits of western dress in addition to a large wardrobe of African costumes of the highest quality fabric and embroidery (cf. Smythe and Smythe, 1960, *passim*; Lloyd (ed.), 1966, *passim*).

To an increasing extent, too, the latter families either occupy land and quarters previously reserved for the European officials, or they have moved to new residential suburbs, several miles from the older part of the town. The result is that different urban areas can roughly be graded according to the socio-economic characteristics of the household units they contain as well as in terms of quality and distribution of public health facilities and the extent to which such districts are planned and developed. As indicated earlier, this tendency was already evident even in colonial times, especially in the Congo. It was Belgian policy there to regulate urban immigration and to discourage tribal identification, and so *parcelles* of land were allocated on the basis of what the Africans allowed to settle were in a position to pay. In other countries the spatial separation of the urban population according to earnings results from the 'ordinary' operation of social and economic forces as well as the special provision made for persons in the administration. For example, in Ibadan there is the 'Old City' where, in 1967, a rough estimate of the average family income was between £50 and £100 per annum; in the Newer Residential Area between 'Old Ibadan' and the suburbs the average annual incomes ranged approximately between £200 and £1,500; and in the Residential Area around the periphery of the city, average annual income ranged between £350 and £3,000 (Okediji and Okediji, 1966; Mabogunje, 1967; Okediji, F. O., 1967; La Fontaine, 1970).

The result of these differences in spending power, residential patterns and the rest is that the urban population tends to be divided into three or four socio-economic strata, whose composition naturally varies a good deal according to the particular town's size and general significance for the national economic and political system. Thus, there will be a considerable difference between the so-called primate city which serves as the nation's capital and, say, mere urban agglomerations which, though populous, have only a single specific function in respect, perhaps, of mining operations.[1] Nevertheless, taking the former type of city for purposes of a model, first will come the men who hold ministerial rank in the government, the judges and the highest ranks in the civil service. These – as indicated above – are the 'new élite' because they have inherited political power from the former colonial administration, and the members of this category have generally had university as well as high school training. In addition, recent military *coups* have, in several countries, brought army officers to the fore. Also politically influential are, in some cases, the well-established landowning lineages, whose heads often possess hereditary titles as traditional rulers. These families continue to be important mainly because of their personal following among the indigenous inhabitants of the town and the villages surrounding it. They set standards that accord with the people's own conception of life and with their traditional values. For related reasons, the principal emirs and other leaders of the Moslem community – the Khalifas of the great sects, the Imams

44

and the men with the title of Al Hadji – are also to be included in this category (Little, 1965, pp. 138–9).

In addition – speaking of the West African region – there are the 'old' families, who in the British territories possessed wealth and position long before Independence. As already indicated, their earlier members served in the colonial legislature, were frequently prosperous enough to have their sons and daughters educated overseas, and were usually the first Africans to practise at the bar. Principally in Senegal, some of the earlier French *évolués* had an analogous position. These particular groups, including families of Sierra Leonean and 'Brazilian' extraction, have generally continued their close connection with Britain and France. The result, since their descendants are usually more at home than other Africans with the niceties of European bourgeois behaviour (see later paragraph), is that these men and women are also to be numbered among the élite (*ibid.*). Other members of the well-to-do class closely associated with the élite are professional men and (sometimes) women, university teachers, prosperous businessmen, less successful politicians, and the senior civil service in general. These are followed by the rank and file of teachers and nurses, clergy, owners of independent businesses, and holders of less important traditional titles. In turn come the junior clerks, artisans, tradesmen, and semi-skilled workers in general, while the broad mass of petty traders, manual workers, market women, messengers and other semi-literate and illiterate inhabitants of the town bring up the rear (*ibid.*).

Income is decided, of course, mainly by occupation and so there are, in the above differentiation, the ingredients of a class system. This is the more evident because the criteria of prestige adduced are closely interrelated. Thus, wealth, needed for purposes of conspicuous consumption, is gained largely through political position which partly depends, in turn, on education. Education itself being of general importance, the more advanced the educational qualification (for example, a university degree), the higher a person is rated. Furthermore, to have studied overseas makes him a 'been-to', eligible automatically for a 'senior service' post, and so completes the circle. The significance of this point is exemplified by Goldthorpe's study (1955, pp. 31–47) of fifty-five former students of Makerere College, then a secondary school. Makerere (now Uganda's university) has been the leading educational institution in

45

East Africa, and Goldthorpe found that forty-three out of his sample were in government or quasi-government employment. Most of them occupied positions that involved a good deal of responsibility. Moreover, as long ago as the 1930s, about 80 per cent of the fathers of these old students were literate (*ibid*, pp. 31–47; see also Goldthorpe, 1956, pp. 115–22).

The unlettered person is also alive to the advantages of education – it can be a means to a larger income and a more comfortable life – but he is not necessarily moved by the spiritual and other non-tangible benefits education is supposed to confer. Consequently, while respecting the educated man's acquisition of western knowledge and skills, he does not feel that educated people are his superiors in any intrinsic sense of the term. Indeed, he is inclined to scoff at and regard as faddish the imitation of some western customs – such as a hygienic regard for health and treatment of food and water (Little, 1967b, p. 261). What he does chiefly admire about the educated person's 'civilized' ways is his possession of fine clothes, better housing and larger supply of manufactured goods. In other words, as a report on Ghanaian 'working class' individuals confirms, the amount of money earned is important. It is this[2] which largely determines the place of the group in the lower as well as the higher social hierarchy, and the amount of earnings is determined by the average education required by each member of the particular occupation or vocation (Ackah, 1969).

However, although a great deal of emphasis is placed upon money, the white-collar and professional occupations are often valued for their own sake, not only because they are usually better paid and carry with them some power and influence. Rather is it because in taking over from the colonialists, Africans have inherited several western social insignia. Consequently, these occupations are preferred because they are similar to those held by Europeans; and so, 'in addition to becoming a criteria of evaluation in a status system, occupation has become a symbol of it'. This is the opinion of Schwab (1961, pp. 139–40) who found in Rhodesia a specific esteem for western occupation, dress, furniture, etiquette, language and leisure activities as well as education. An educated man was thought to have knowledge of the 'civilized way of life', and relatively high educational qualifications were symbolic of prestige and a requisite of high status. Yet, despite these considerations it is premature, in Schwab's opinion, to speak of a full-fledged class system among Africans in Rhodesia, and Mitchell's view of Northern Rhodesia (now Zambia) is apparently similar. He and Epstein found among urban Africans a fairly clear-cut system of prestige based on the outward marks of western civilization. This scale clearly affected interpersonal relationships among Africans in towns, but it did not yet provide a basis for the recruitment of corporately acting groups (Mitchell and Epstein, 1959, pp. 22–40).[3]

Nor is such a basis likely to come into existence so long as African family groups remain closely knit. A university graduate holding an important government post may have a brother who is a subsistence farmer, another who is an unskilled labourer, and a sister who is married to a primary teacher. He will see all of them more or less regularly and such occupational heterogeneity is widespread. Thus, Peil's enquiries among Ghanaian factory workers disclosed that in most cases the worker had at least as much education as others in his family, but a substantial minority of workers had siblings who had gone beyond them in school or who had gone to school when they had not. Several had brothers who were in universities abroad and who would soon return to Ghana as professionals (Peil, 1972, pp. 51–2).

The drawback, therefore, to a class formulation is, as Schwab has pointed out, that the structure of 'the stratification system is extremely amorphous'. This is because in the general heterogeneity of urban life the valuation of what is socially regarded as worthwhile is diffuse and ill-defined. It is blurred, on the one hand, by traditional ideas of status and etiquette, and complicated, on the other, by educated people being accorded specific remarks of precedence. They may, for example, be sheltered from the crowd by the police, given chairs and placed in the front at public functions, etc. Nor is their own attitude always consistent, because there is evidence of élite individuals founding recreational associations of their own which are exclusive. This happened – according to Plotnicov – in Jos on the Nigerian Plateau, when the social club to which the élite section belonged opened its doors to Africans whom it regarded as unlettered and uncouth (1970, pp. 295–6). Other clubs insist on 'civilized' standards of dress and deportment being observed (see also Little, 1955b). Indeed, except to the extent that it is necessary for politics or business, some individuals deliberately eschew social contact with illiterate people (cf. Gamble, 1963).

This kind of person does not join a 'traditional' association and

47

he would probably not allow his wife to trade in the market or own a bar. But there are others – the headmaster of a school, for instance – who do not think it odd for their wives to earn money in this way (Little, 1965, pp. 142–3). In fact, in Ghana, it is claimed (Ackah, 1969, p. 6) that:

> Every member of the community, from the head of state to the conservancy cleaner, can go to any shop anywhere . . . and he or she will be served in the same way as any other person. At weddings and parties and convivialities . . . guests do range from high class to the low class people. When people talk of society weddings, one often sees clerks and even messengers and others of like status among the guests. . . .
>
> I know of several instances of heads of departments or top managers of firms having as guests at Christmas parties members of their staff from the top to the bottom. Not even the general drinks parties that are given by the head of state on great occasions are confined to top men and women. There is always a sprinkling of clerks and other working class people, which is a simple way of showing that a citizen is a citizen, whatever his social status.

On the other hand, while arguing that there are only a few individuals holding responsible positions who may be 'generally snobbish', Ackah concedes that 'the social classes are there'. Thus, unless one is a well-to-do cocoa farmer, to exchange a rural for an urban occupation seems to betoken an advance as does movement from messenger to factory worker. The latter also ranks higher than ordinary workers; but, as implied above, the reason why social distance between clerks and intelligentsia is even greater is mainly cultural.

The male and female members of the westernized élite meet regularly at public functions and visit each other's homes for cocktails. To the extent that they share the same way of life and the same set of business, political, professional and other interests, this group constitutes a separate class and even a community of its own. These people, as observation of the Nigerian situation has shown, have discarded the provincialism of the average individual. Their interest in times and places beyond the awareness of the masses, and their respect for scientific reason and analysis as opposed to supernatural explanations of natural phenomena, are important factors drawing them together and creating a sense of corporateness and solidarity (Smythe and Smythe, 1960, p. 93; Little, 1965, pp. 151–2). Indeed, according to Plotnicov, the élite's skilful command of European behaviour patterns is directed toward other Africans. It not only confers prestige on these who possess the requisite qualifications, it also serves to prevent entrance to and dilution of the élite stratum by parvenus and unacceptable élite aspirants (Plotnicov, 1970, pp. 295–6).[4]

Apart, however, from these relatively well-to-do and well-educated people, there is no one focus for sentiment or unitary system of values in modern African towns. True, both settled inhabitants and migrants have a common interest in making money and improving their material position. This is the principal reason which prompted the latter's movement, but even prolonged residence in a town atmosphere does not necessarily alter their attitude. It does not automatically change country-bred people and convert them into true townsmen. In other words, there are circumstances in which urbanization as defined earlier stops short and does not apply at all to certain sections of the town's population.

Lunsar in Sierra Leone provides a significant illustration of this point, because its present inhabitants were attracted there almost entirely by opportunities of work in a nearby iron-ore mine. As a result, not only is Lunsar's population of some 15,000 multi-tribal, but nearly all these people are first- or second-generation migrants. The Temne, the principal tribe represented, come from rural villages, where the way of life is based on subsistence rice farming. Traditionally, there is a clan system, and people live domestically in extended families, venerate ancestral spirits, and believe in the existence of genii and bush spirits. The Temne living in Lunsar, however, have given up most of these practices. They take jobs at the mine or earn money in other ways. Mostly, their family units are small; they occupy rented housing and the children are encouraged to do well at school. In the main, therefore, although some traditional customs persist, the Temne show general readiness to assimilate to urban and industrial conditions. Their aspirations are set in a western direction, and many belong to Christian churches. Those who have well-paid jobs at the mine take pride in furnishing their homes in modern style, and they regard monogamy as the proper form of marriage (cf. Gamble, 1963, *passim*).

This is also the general trend in Lunsar, but Fulbe[5] migrants constitute an exception (Butcher, 1964). These people move to Lunsar from Guinea where historically they were the aristocratic overlords of Futa Jallon. This supremacy was gained by fighting, and it involved a caste system. The Fulbe are also strict Moslems and sufficiently proud of their religion to look down upon non-Moslems; other Africans who are Christians or animists they affect to despise. Fulbe migrants carry this outlook to Lunsar, where their community is stratified, the main strata consisting respectively of the freeborn, the praise singers, the blacksmiths and the slaves. This means that a Pullo arriving in Lunsar is not a complete stranger. Even though he has no kin or friends there, he is allotted a position according to the status he held in the Futa Jallon (*ibid.*).

It follows from this situation that, despite migration, the older way and habits are maintained. Fulbe teachers indoctrinate the young with Fulbe history and myth, and children are sent to an *alfa* or *karamoko*. From him they learn to write a little Arabic and Pullo, but they are not allowed to attend a primary school because such schools are run by Christian missions. Without a primary school education, it is impossible to go to a government high school; hence very few Fulbe have any formal education or training in western skills. The mine is the main source of employment in Lunsar, but being qualified only to perform menial tasks, the free-born Fulbe do not apply there for work. That would mean accepting jobs they regard as degrading and beneath their dignity. Instead, most Fulbe follow traditional occupations, such as cattle trading, and, fortified by their religion and conscious of their distinctive outlook and occupation, hold themselves aloof from the other inhabitants of Lunsar. Many such Fulbe have rooms or houses there but they take a little or no part in its modern institutions and activities (*ibid.*).[6]

Some authors have described an attitude such as the above as 'supertribalism' and the Zabrama who have moved to Ghana from Niger provide a further example. These people are not numerous in Accra and the other towns but the typical Zabrama migrant is a single man, or, if he is married, he sends his wife back to his home country. Although remaining faithful to their relations with other groups of migrants, to their old enmities and old alliances, these Zabrama exiles take no part in traditional local life except to pay homage to the chief at the *Odwira* celebrations and on the other civic occasions. Instead, they transplant as far as possible the social systems of their own country, including sub-district and village communities which do not allow the migrant to leave this entirely Zabrama milieu throughout his whole stay. Indeed, this tendency to isolate themselves exists from the start because the migrants entering Ghana from the north are, from their departure, members of a single group. If, on their arrival, this group disperses, it is only to form other groups in different places of residence – a process which is encouraged by high rentals and housing shortages. Consequently, a small room will be shared between three, five or ten men, and obviously these room-mates are always people of the same origin – from the same district if not the same village.[7] The room thus becomes – in Rouch's graphic language – 'a little regional cell' where one takes one's meals in common and where, in the evenings after work, one talks endlessly of one's country. Rouch suggests that this talking at night, *takaneya*, is just as necessary in a sordid shack as in a rural village (Rouch, 1954, pp. 56, 60).

Equally 'incapsulated' in similar terms are Xhosa migrants studied by Philip Mayer (1961, pp. 61–4) in the South African town of East London. Known as the 'Red' people because of their custom of wearing a red blanket, this particular section of the tribe insists on remaining typically pagan and illiterate. Xhosa men in general seek urban employment as a matter of course, but unlike 'Mission' and 'School' products of the same ethnic group, most of these Red people steadfastly refuse to internalize the values of white civilization.

Unlike the Zabrama, who are hundreds of miles from their home-land, the Xhosa move to a city lying so close to the rural hinterland that they can make brief visits there during their prolonged stay in town. In this case, therefore, it is the very proximity of the migrants' villages which encourages exclusiveness because in Mayer's opinion it is this home visiting which helps to keep the 'Red' type of man faithfully 'Red' during all his years in town. He continues to be bound to one specific 'Red' family, lineage, and community in the country. Also, like the Zabrama, the Red Xhosa migrant restricts himself as far as possible to the company of home friends, residing with them and spending all his leisure time with these fellow exiles from his own place. The result is that on returning to his rural village, a Red man can fit in almost as if he had not been away (Mayer, 1961, pp. 94ff.).

In each of the above cases the migrants concerned retain to a

51

considerable extent their traditional culture and outlook. They reside in the town, but for most of them the place in which they work or do their business is not a permanent home. Instead, while working abroad the migrants – the Tonga mentioned above are a typical example – send back money to wives and relatives with which to buy clothes, pay fines and bridewealth and even to purchase food. In return for these and other services the man who is away expects his kinsfolk at home to protect his membership of and his place in rural society. Consequently, for the latter type of migrant, the town in which they do their business is not regarded in any sense as 'home'. They may own property there, may make repeated visits, spend part of many years in it, but without acquiring any feeling of attachment. As explained of the Tonga in Chapter 1, their social selves remain safeguarded in their villages, among their lineage people there. Only in an economic sense do they take part in the town's social system.

True, as already indicated, there are 'School' migrants from the same tribe who assimilate readily to the town's social institutions including clubs, associations and churches, as well as to industrial conditions of employment. Also, as Chapter 6 will show, 'adaptive mechanisms' are at work which effectively assist urbanization and provide all the stimulation needed. However, letting this point go; the situation just described is omnipresent and significant enough to make the urban process a matter of segmentation as well as social differentiation. In other words, although there is in the industrialized town's social structure a pattern of stratification, the part played additionally by ethnic, tribal or religious affiliation is, sometimes, of even greater importance. This means that on the one hand the mixing of members of different ethnic groups has increased so that the ties between people of the same socio-economic class are being strengthened. On the other, since it is membership of a given ethnic group which also determines the amount of prestige a man can win in society at large,[8] there are occasions when a person prefers to conceive of himself in the first place as an African, Indian, European, or, again, as a Moslem or Christian, or as a Ganda or a Luo. Whether he identifies in this way rather than as a member of a social class depends on how he defines the given social situation and whether he is brought structurally into opposition to another group.[9] Thus, in Mombasa (Kenya), for example, a wealthy Ismaeli is likely to have closer face-to-face relationships with poor Ismaelis than with people who, although on his own economic level, are ethnically different (Southall, 1961, p. 40).

Furthermore – as studies of the Fulbe, the Tonga and the 'Red' Xhosa have indicated – this point becomes progressively significant as literacy decreases, and a member of the élite who needs his fellow tribesmen's support generally pays heed to this. He knows that, although he may have gained certain western symbols of success, he must continue, at the same time, to conform with traditional ideas of the 'big man'. This will involve keeping open house and entertaining all and sundry. It will mean that although this person, Mr X, may drive around in his Mercedes with other professional people and drink with them at his club, he will remember his kinship obligations. However poor or illiterate his own or his wife's relatives, there must always be room for them in his house or compound. His westernized wife, too, must defer to the older people. On her visits to his natal compound she may be expected to wear her oldest *lappa* and perform with alacrity the customary obeisances and chores (Bird, n.d.; Little, 1965, pp. 142–3).

The situation described above involves considerations of both 'class' and 'ethnicity' and illustrates specifically what opportunism means in sociological terms. It amounts, in essence, to an ability not only to move smoothly between one social system and another; but to manipulate – as the occasion arises – either system to one's own purposes. Thus, in the circumstances depicted above, if Mr X has ambitions as a politician he must design his behaviour to suit the expectations of two different sets of potential supporters. There will be those educated people who, like himself, conceive of government as being based on a relatively 'rational' set of political aims and a given party programme, and the more traditionally-minded element whose political universe is circumscribed by accustomed allegiances to ethnic group, tribe, and kinsfolk. Since to the latter group customary ideas of status are more important than abstract ideals of 'democracy', 'socialism', etc., the would-be political leader must get his priorities right. He needs to proceed according to principles of what has been termed 'situational selection'; and Achebe's account of the *arriviste* Federal Minister, 'Chief Nanga's', visit to his rural constituents provides an illuminative example of this. The fact that one of their own sons has attained high office is a source of considerable gratification to these villagers. They greet their 'big man' tumultuously; but what puts the complete seal on their approval of 'Nanga' is his deference to the reception committee's older members. In Achebe's words (1966, pp. 11–12):

> The crowd raised a deafening shout of welcome. [Chief Nanga] waved his fan to the different parts of the hall. Then he turned to Mr Nwege and said:
> 'Thank you very much, thank you, sir.'
> A huge, tough-looking member of the Minister's entourage who stood with us at the back of the dais raised his voice and said:
> 'You see wetin I de talk. How many minister fit hanswer *Sir* to any Tom, Dick and Harry, way senior them for age? Mark you how many?'
> Everyone at the dais agreed that the Minister was quite exceptional in this respect – a man of high position who still gave age the respect due to it. . . .

In short, the result is that the educated African is often called upon to move in two social worlds, involving in several respects quite different norms of conduct and behaviour. The kind of behaviour expected of him varies with the nature of the situation and the situation itself is mainly defined by the extent to which 'western' agencies – in the persons of Europeans or other well-educated Africans, or institutions such as a school or government or modern business office – are involved. This means that at work or at church or at an official reception, for example, he behaves in a 'modern' way. In his own home and family circle his actions may be, partly at least, 'traditional' and geared to traditional requirements.[10] This is another way of saying, though at the cost of considerable simplification,[11] that in his private life he is an 'African', in public a 'Westerner' (cf. Little, 1955a, p. 231).

5

Urbanization and race relations

We ended the last chapter with a quotation illustrating not only characteristic 'ploys' of an opportunistic society, but one of the ways in which the effects of an urban-centred institution – party politics – 'ripples out' into the countryside. Of course, the interplay of modern and traditional aims and interests has significance as well for even more basic institutions of marriage and family. The latter subject will be duly considered, but in the meantime the segmentation described above raises the question of pluralism.[1] In other words, how far is it helpful to conceive of the urban social structure as being constituted from a multiplicity of autonomous but interdependent groups? True, there are also countervailing forces at work, but the pluralistic formulation has roots in the colonial as well as the indigenous situations. In the latter, for example, it is a matter of pronounced cleavages between African units of the urban population, which involve age-old enmities and alliances. One of the most obvious in Ghana is the hostility of the Zabramas and the Gaos against the Hausas, and the friendship between the Moshies and the Zabramas; the Fulani are not popular with any group. These groups regard themselves as Moslems, but Islam is not strong enough alone to override these differences and so the migrants have only one thing in common: they are foreigners. As such they are shunned by the indigenous inhabitants for whom any migrant is straightaway assimilated with the natives of the Northern Territories: he is a 'bushman', a naked barbarian. The migrants retort in similar terms and refer to the people of the Coast as 'sons of slaves' (Rouch, 1954, pp. 59, 62).[2] More dramatically and tragically, too, the recent Nigerian civil war had its basis largely in relations of hostility between the Ibo and the Hausa.

55

These are all instances of the divisive processes of 'ethnicity' but a further species, writ even larger and more widely, tends to be the racial relationships between black and white. This aspect of pluralism – if we accept the concept[3] – derives from the attitudes used to justify colonialism itself. Africans, it was argued, were incapable of competing with Europeans in a modern technically advanced era; hence they were the 'white man's burden'. The latter, being responsible for the coloured races' welfare, had the right to order and control their affairs. If he considered that contact with white civilization was inimical to Africans, then their segregation and exclusion from western education and skills was the moral as well as the logical policy. This kind of reasoning is explicit in South Africa, but it was also implicit in colonies with an ostensibly liberal policy where the presence of the anopheles mosquito impeded European settlement. In the latter West African countries, European domination was rationalized instead in terms of *trustee-ship*, the white man being the 'trustee' and the African his 'ward'.

Oliver Cromwell Cox has categorized the latter type of race relations as the ruling-class situation because the Europeans in control constituted a tiny minority. They consisted mostly of civil servants, were drawn from the highly educated sections of the metropolitan population and maintained an attitude of paternalism towards the Africans. Since the overwhelming mass of the latter lived in the countryside, there was very little contact between the races. Virtually, every administrator was European and the only places where Africans and Europeans met were in government offices, mission stations, and in business and industry. Almost invariably these Africans were in subordinate positions, the only important exception being the very small African 'middle class' of western-educated people mentioned above who, in the British colonies, sometimes included prosperous merchants, doctors and lawyers with seats in the legislative councils.

The French, as mentioned, singled out their *évolués* for social privileges but British policy was more discriminatory. It deliberately kept virtually all Africans at a distance and involved a more conscious sense of racial solidarity, whose most obvious and outward form was the exclusive European club. Solidarity was also symbolically expressed in regalia and ritual. The higher the individual status the greater the formality,[4] and at the top were members of the political or administrative service,[5] followed, in approximate order, by those in the legal and medical branches, police, education, agriculture, forestry, customs, post and telegraph, public works and railway.[6] A person's position in this hierarchy also decided his membership of the various clubs which, in addition to excluding Africans, differentiated between Europeans themselves. Thus, while the government club consisted entirely of higher civil servants and their peers, technicians working on the railway automatically belonged to another.[7]

These differences in status were naturally reflected in differences in living standards and Europeans' residential quarter with its neatly trimmed gardens and spacious bungalows was impressive. Trees and hedges concealed their domestic lives but Africans working as 'house boys' reported on the luxuries enjoyed, including comfortable furniture and a supply of modern appliances. Not that this kind of wealth necessarily excited envy. Many rural migrants were accustomed to their own rulers and big men living in relative opulence,[8] and the fact that Europeans were materially very much better off and of a different race did not bother the *illiterate* migrant or townsman. He looked upon their socially and economically superior position in the same way as he regarded his own rulers and chiefs, taking for granted the European's scientific knowledge and highly advanced technology as the source of his power. Consequently, instead of European paternalism being resented it was, to traditionally minded Africans, simply a mark of status; indeed, something with which they were already familiar and regarded as right and proper.[9]

With urbanization, however, the basis for a different pattern of racial relationships was laid. This happened because the expansion of commerce and industry referred to above necessitated in West Africa a much enlarged supply of literate and educated workers; not only semi-skilled and unskilled labour but men, and even women, at all educational levels. Schools were built to cater for this demand, the result being that more and more young people were introduced to the values of urban society, including the incentive to live in a 'civilized' way. This, as already explained, encouraged the desire for wage-employment; but the important thing was that even a few years at school were enough to thrust many of the individuals on to the fringe of a new society. This meant not only that a regular supply of cash had to be earned or gained in whatever way was possible, but that personal achievement was now measured and goals set in terms of the urban system. It meant that, unlike their illiterate compatriots, this section of African society took Europeans as their reference group. They sought, in other words, to emulate European living standards, and when the Europeans argued that eligibility for promotion required higher educational and technical qualifications, the Africans so motivated duly studied hard and rapidly filled the places available to upwardly mobile men. This left an overflow of occupationally and socially ambitious people who considered that they were on the last rung permitted them and that they needed to be free of discrimination in order to climb higher (Hanna, 1963, p. 14).

Numerous party leaders were ready to take up this cause but their appeal tended to be limited to their fellow ethnics. Something had to be done to overcome such sectionalism and so it became the practice in the interests of African unity to stigmatize not only the government but Europeans as a group.[10]   For example, the late Kwame Nkrumah, taking 'Pan-Africanism'[11] as his platform, claimed that 'Europeans relegated us to the position of inferiors in every respect of our everyday life' (Hanna, 1963, p. 13), while a Zikist[12] pamphlet issued in 1950 not only exhorted Africans to 'revolt', it also declared – 'you should hate every European in this country' (Olusanya, op. cit.). Feelings of this kind were not confined to politicians because four-fifths of Jahoda's informants thought that whites had a poor opinion of Africans.[13]

In this way the ideas that Africans and Europeans had of each other gradually became racist in character, involving the use of stereotypes on both sides. For example, African employment of the term 'expatriate' signified that the European to whom it was applied had been imported into the country to take jobs which an African could do as well, if not better. Europeans, on their part, were generally much more tolerant of the so-called 'bush' African than of his literate or educated compatriot. The former's 'simple ways' and 'good manners' were approved, whereas the 'urban' African was stigmatized as 'lazy', 'corrupt' and 'pushing'. Europeans tended to be particularly patronizing of any African who 'attempted' (as it was put) to emulate European etiquette and social symbols,[14] while they denigrated at the same time those educated Africans who continued to observe traditional custom by living in a family compound, eating in traditional fashion, and so on. The latter were spoken of as 'reverting to type' or as being 'incapable of learning better' (Little, 1955a, pp. 274–7), and the extreme view was that as persons Africans hardly existed at all.[15]

So much for attitudes in the Anglophone territories. The French, by contrast, were less tolerant of the rural population and were antagonistic rather than sympathetic towards traditional customs. However, even the paternalism which they showed towards Africans who 'learned to be French'[16] changed when, especially after the Second World War, large numbers of emigrants arrived from France itself seeking employment in Afrique Occidentale Française. In those territories as a whole the French population grew by 125 per cent between 1946 and 1951 and, in Dakar – the AOF's 'capital city' – it multiplied six times between 1938 and 1955. As explained, Dakar's European population originally consisted essentially of cadres in positions of command, technical direction and so on. The new influx altered this entire occupational structure by introducing in addition to the characteristically colonial hierarchy of top civil servants and army officers and upper echelons of commercial and banking companies[17] a European 'lower middle class'. Not only did this comprise manual workers, artisans and NCO's, but even a group of poor whites appeared.[18] These people wanted the same kind of work for which there were now growing numbers of Africans educated enough to perform. The result was that although the government tried to provide enough jobs for all, competition between the new African *petite bourgeoisie* and the *petits blancs* (as they were called) grew increasingly strong[19] and was reflected in the racist attitudes which soon developed among the less favoured French categories. Such prejudices were markedly different from those of the older colonialists. They disapproved of racial intolerance being overtly displayed; but the result, nevertheless, was an increasing gap between Europeans and Africans in all social classes. This happened because the *modus vivendi* governing previous African-European relationships failed to survive the urban realities of a different order.

Thus, whereas the original settlement found in all coastal towns of Senegal was not divided into racial sections, new and exclusively European residential zones now took shape, arguments about hygiene being used to justify separation. And so, little by little, the 'European town' created its own services, and the illegality of indiscriminatory practices did not prevent some hotels, bars and cafés ensuring an exclusively European patronage for themselves.

Paradoxically, too, although cultural differences between the African *bourgeoisie* and the Europeans were actually diminishing, the social distance between them became wider. Mercier, for example, found that over three-quarters of the European respondents he studied had never associated, even occasionally, with an African outside their place of work and less than 2 per cent of them had ever had African friends. The highest rate of racial interaction seemed to prevail among persons in the politically militant left wing, but it was also among the economically less well-off Europeans that tensions were the most violent (Mercier, 1955).

Significant, therefore, in the development of racial separation and antagonism in Dakar was the fact that changes in *both* groups took place. Not only did the European settlement increase in size and alter in social composition, but there was also increased urbanization on the African side. Since this involved, in turn, greater participation of Africans within the same social structure as Europeans (Mercier, 1955, pp. 283–304),[20] it brought Europeans and Africans into collision.

How far has the situation been altered by Independence? This, it would appear, brought into being an ideal formulation of co-operation between French and Senegalese which took the concrete form of technical and financial assistance to the new all-African government. However, when in 1966–7 Rita Cruise O'Brien studied the effects, she found that although 65 per cent of some 250 French residents interviewed by her considered contact with Africans to be important, it was only in the upper middle class and, to some extent, the middle class circles, that there was any appreciable amount of mixing outside the office, workshop or factory. Most of this, too, was purely formal in character and did not extend much further than official receptions, diplomatic parties and joint membership of some élite social clubs and voluntary associations. Moreover, there was an obvious discrepancy between French attitudes 'for public consumption' and what was said behind the closed doors of a French sitting room after dinner. Although, in the latter context, some French people expressed interest in and a desire to meet Africans on terms of social equality, most comments were very derogatory. The Senegalese were widely considered to be either biologically or culturally inferior, and there was a particular contempt for the African élite (1972, pp. 20–1, 239–60).

Senegalese attitudes, on the other hand, appeared to be both more ambivalent and even paradoxical. Thus, although those furthest from Europeans in terms of social distance and education were least critical,[21] stereotypical views of Frenchmen were found less frequently among Senegalese with a relatively high educational achievement, especially when such people had lived in France itself. On the whole, although a fairly high proportion of O'Brien's respondents seemed to hold a not unfavourable view of the French in general, there were very evident undertones of antagonism. Thus, although it was admitted that a proportion of the French tried to be 'communicative' and were 'correct' in their behaviour, an antipathetic minority of the Senegalese obviously regarded them as being racist at heart.[22]

Taking this and the fact of cultural differences into account it would appear that, in effect, Senegalese and French live side by side largely as separate communities. For the Senegalese as well as the French there is a kind of 'public code' of co-operation in the multiracial field and a corresponding lack of overt racism.[23] Perhaps, therefore, the main difference made by Independence is that not only are the Senegalese now politically in charge but that separation is for the greater part by mutual consent. That the latter is the case seems to be reflected most sharply in a more or less mutual rejection of inter-marriage because, if the evidence presented by O'Brien can be taken at its face value, neither side is eager to encourage assimilation. Numbers of such marriages, mainly between educated Senegalese and French women of middle or lower middle class, have taken place, but even the small minority of Senegalese and French who approve of the idea of mixed unions often have reservations (pp. 266–73).

In moving on to compare recent developments in the Anglophone countries it is necessary to stress the long-standing position of Dakar and other towns as places where fairly substantial numbers of French people settled in order to carry on business. The British, by contrast, had much less to lose through African political and economic development. They went to Ghana, Nigeria and the other colonial territories as employees of the government, the missions, industry and commerce, and merely served one or more tours of duty. West Africa was not in any sense their home, and newcomers, moreover, arriving after the Second World War were mostly employed on a few years' contract, while for European civil servants compulsorily 'retired' there was generous compensation or the opportunity of a post elsewhere. Once the British had decided to transfer power, these circumstances facilitated the policy of rapid 'Africanization' referred to in the last chapter. 'Africanization' not only involved the appointment of some Africans as heads of government departments and the upgrading of many others, but the placing of Africans in ministerial positions. Also, although Europeans continued to direct many offices, schools and hospitals, more and more Africans worked with them as colleagues. This, in turn, brought Africans and Europeans socially together at the élite level of society spoken of above. It meant that African and European senior civil servants met for formal dinners; and dining clubs consisting of African and European women also came into existence. Thus, in Anglophone West Africa an incipient racial problem was nipped in the bud, even though some conservative European circles felt that fraternization should be kept well within bounds and not carried beyond the demand of official policy and ordinary courtesy. But it was no less significant that numbers of Europeans of both sexes had close personal relationships with Africans and seemed to have no difficulty in mixing freely with them.[24]

During this transitional period, much depended on Europeans at the top and in one of the higher civil servants' clubs the attitude of the European brigadier in charge of the local army detachment appears to have been decisive. A number of his officers were Africans and he let it be understood that he himself would resign if they were not made equally eligible for membership. In the European 'Railway' Club, on the other hand, resistance was stiffer. Its members were largely men on the lowest grade, including permanent way inspectors who supervised the maintenance of track and senior locomotive foremen who maintained engines.[25] Objections to African membership were eventually waived, partly because the Governor of the colony himself showed that he personally disapproved of the club's discrimination,[26] and a rumour also went round that the club would be deprived of its land unless the door was opened to Africans. There was a last-ditch stand by the more conservative element but a small number of socially acceptable Africans were admitted and the colour bar was broken (Proudfoot and Wilson, 1961).[27]

In other words, relations tend to be less easy when Europeans working as technicians, such as building contractors or foremen, are involved. They have generally little to do with Africans except in their capacity as subordinates or servants and resent the university-trained African's higher status. It is, in fact, in the churches, among university circles and in the larger schools with mixed staffs that relationships are least formal and that Europeans and Africans entertain each other in their respective homes, belong to the same associations and join each other at dances and other social gatherings. Also, a fairly large number of marriages have taken place, mainly between African professionals and British middle class women. A few Europeans have African wives, but the custom of keeping an African mistress is still more common. In short, since neither Africans nor Europeans are, as groups, 'colour blind', race relations continue, in the technical sense,[28] to exist. What is lacking is the mutual antipathy, the bitter hostility, suspicion and tension that characterize the southern part of Africa. Racial relations, in other words, do not constitute either a social or a political problem in Anglophone West Africa.

What is the reason for this relatively harmonious situation? As we have explained, there was a period when feelings ran high and both Africans and Europeans were on the verge of mutual hatred and disposed to regard each other racially as out-groups. For the lessening of tension on the British side we have already provided part of the answer, but the fact that Africans are now politically in command is the paramount consideration. It ensures that whatever their actual feelings, Europeans take good care to keep colour prejudice out of sight. They realize that no outright display of racial discrimination will be countenanced and, indeed, more than one European has found himself on the next plane home following something said or done that he himself did not wittingly intend to be racially prejudicial.[29] African governments thus tend sometimes to be ultra-sensitive, especially where white South Africans are concerned. But despite their recent status as colonial subjects, the ordinary man and woman in the street bear little or no animosity towards white people. True, there are some quarters of the town where it might be unwise and even dangerous for a European to walk about alone, but this applies also to Africans who look prosperous enough to be worth robbing. On the whole, therefore, reactions to a white face are friendly, and a European is often made to feel welcome although much will depend upon such a person's status and manner.[30]

63

The reason for this relatively relaxed situation is that even when relations between Africans and Europeans were most strained, Africans retained a considerable respect for European institutions. Thus, unfavourable stereotypes of Europeans were held for a time, but Jahoda's study of African attitudes also found that white people were 'liked' rather than 'disliked', the ratio being almost exactly two to one, i.e. two-thirds 'liking' and one-third 'disliking'. True, this investigation was carried out *after* Ghanaian Independence, and when contacts between Europeans and Africans occurred on a basis of higher versus lower status, of employer versus white-collar or manual worker, the relationship inevitably involved tensions and antagonism rather than friendship. On the other hand, the higher the level of education, the greater the chance of informal meetings and so of a favourable attitude. Thus, only 42 per cent of those who met whites only in their job liked whites, as against 80 per cent of those whose contacts were not thus confined.[31]

In contrast to the Anglophone countries, O'Brien's data cited above suggest an underlying resentment of the European, and both her and Mercier's report indicate that friendly contacts were, and still are, infrequent at all levels. This seems surprising in view of earlier French toleration of at least the *évolué* category. If, then, the latter's relationship with his French counterpart became in the end less, rather than more, easy-going than that of the educated Anglophone African, what was the reason? Possibly it lies in the very conditions that in the British territories originally placed educated Africans at a disadvantage compared with products of the *lycée*. The British did not encourage the African intelligentsia either to be leaders or to regard themselves as anything but 'African'. True, during the nineteenth century Liberated Africans in Sierra Leone were 'Christianized' and 'Westernized' to an extent that merited their description as 'black Englishmen', but Africans in general were not invited to think of themselves as 'British'. They were taught to look up to the United Kingdom and to respect the British Crown, but were not encouraged to assimilate to British culture. This had such peculiar virtues and profundities that only a native-born Briton could hope to understand it. As a result, unlike the situation in Francophone Africa, there being no pressure on the educated African to ape his colonial masters, he could afford to be objective and to select the particular new customs he wanted, thinking of them as 'western' or 'European' rather than 'British'. Purely practical and pragmatic reasons determined his choice and for him there was no mystique or anything intrinsically valuable[32] about the modern institutions he adopted. They happened to order much of the world to which he aspired, and so it was logical to acquire the kind of western technical expertise and know-how needed for his own and his country's advancement.

Consequently, European exclusiveness did not unduly shock the African in the British territories or undermine his self-confidence. He had his kinsfolk and a society of his own to fall back on; and, never having been encouraged to regard himself as anything but 'African', he did not feel betrayed when paternalism turned sour. Certainly, racialism was something to be resented and fought, but the educated African's desire for social equality – for 'freedom from contempt', as he called it – was largely a projection of nationalist ambitions on to the social scene.[33] When these had been realized, previous rebuffs by Europeans could be forgotten, because unlike perhaps the Senegalese *évolués*, he felt no dependence upon the British or their way of life.[34] Certainly, some Africans demanded membership of European clubs, but this was merely to demonstrate their right to join them. In other words, the African's desire for equality was not a desire for social acceptance. Its motivation was political; and so, once Independence had been gained, the manner in which Europeans carried on their affairs was not the African's concern. The important thing was that Africans and not Europeans had charge of the country (Little, 1955b, pp. 263–83).

We have tried in this analysis to show the effect of urbanization on race relations. The interesting and paradoxical thing is that through urbanization the balance of group feelings and attitudes shifted not once but twice. Thus, although previously the European community as an entity was socially differentiated, it was structurally opposed at the same time to Africans as a whole. Racial intermixture was possible, but on the European side social controls of a caste-like nature virtually ruled out intermarriage. Subsequent 'Africanization' did not alter the hierarchical situation as such, but it meant that relationships between Africans and Europeans of the same status were governed henceforth by the same social norms as those which decided relationships between Europeans themselves. For example, in Sierra Leone the Europeans' most socially select club was opened to Africans of commissioned rank, but remained closed to European non-commissioned officers, even warrant officers. The latter could only belong to a socially inferior club which, by this time, also admitted Africans of comparable social status. In other words, racial exclusiveness on both sides gave way to social exclusiveness, meaning that at the top levels of society considerations of 'class' tended to replace those of 'colour'.

Finally, although no analysis of the connection of urbanization with race is complete without southern Africa,[35] it must suffice to end this already lengthy chapter with a lesser known but not unimportant phenomenon belonging to the same broad category. This is the position of 'minority groups', such as Indians in East Africa and Lebanese in West Africa. These communities constitute less than 2 per cent of the total population of the regions they inhabit;[36] nevertheless, their presence is sociologically significant for urbanization for two reasons. First, it was largely Indian labour and initiative that made European settlement itself possible in East Africa, especially in the shape of 'modern' towns.[37] Secondly, the Indians' position *vis-à-vis* Africans can be seen historically as a function of the racial system forecast by Sir Harry Johnston. His belief was that tropical Africa, between the Zambezi and the Atlas, must be ruled by Whites, developed by Indians, and worked by Blacks (cf. Banton, 1967, p. 212).

In fact, the situation had its origin in the 'Swahili' coast referred to earlier, where small numbers of Indians had lived for many centuries. Mostly they dealt in slaves, but rarely ventured upcountry themselves. When, however, the railways were built colonies of those merchants moved inland at once and were joined, in turn, by enterprising friends and relatives who saw an opportunity of providing trades and skills which the Africans could not supply. Mostly these immigrants came from Gujerati-speaking areas of north-west India and they were mainly petty traders and artisans. Unlike, therefore, the unskilled 'coolies' imported into southern Africa and other territories of the then colonial world they possessed some education.[38] This naturally gave them an advantage for the essentially urban role they were to perform,[39] including their special and successful participation in commerce. Thus, in the 1950s, for example, nearly half of the Indians resident in Uganda were in wholesale or retail trade. However, an additional reason for Indians remaining heavily concentrated in towns was government policy which debarred them from acquiring land rights, except in leasehold urban property. By preventing landlordism, this legislation compelled Indians to invest their surplus in expanding business, lending money on goods or credit, or in other enterprises (Morris, 1956, pp. 194–211).

Moreover, although divided between Hindus and Moslems – including many different castes and sects – the Indians retained their own cultural habits and languages as well as religion and, until recent years, made little or no attempt to assimilate to the 'host' African society. For example, instead of the men marrying Africans, wives were brought from India as also were husbands when in due course girls of the Africa-born generation began to grow up. In other words, the Indians' orientation remained steadfastly towards India itself. It was relatively easy to travel backwards and forwards and so social relationships with the family at home were not broken off. Rather were the young people sent back there to complete their education (Morris, 1956); and although some of it was involuntary, separation was encouraged by residential segregation which continues to persist. For example, a recent study in Juja – a middle-class area of Nairobi – found that Asians, mostly Indians, occupied some 87 per cent of the building plots (Tiwari, 1972).

These marked symptoms of ethnicity, coupled with the Indians' relative prosperity and modern 'know-how', explain how they came to occupy a distinctive as well as intermediate position between the European rulers and the African masses. However, although the latter attributes consolidated the Indians as a species of middle class between European rulers and African peasantry, they also made them highly vulnerable when the racial hierarchy ceased to be under British control. In other words, antipathy and antagonism between Africans and Indians, mostly dormant during colonial rule, were brought to the surface when Independence altered the order of racial status.

Racial stereotypes played a large part in this hostility and their role is shown by Sofer's study of relationships between Africans and Asians in the developing Ugandan town of Jinja (1956, pp. 590–612). This was in 1951 and at that time Jinja's population of some 21,000 persons included some 15,000 Africans, 1,000 Europeans and some 5,000 Asians, of whom almost all the younger ones had been born in Uganda and most of their parents in India. The majority of African earners in Jinja were manual workers and in a sample of 100 such male labourers, Sofer found that 45 were un-skilled and a further 25 semi-skilled or artisans.[40] Among the Asians, on the other hand, about 30 per cent were businessmen, 23 per cent skilled artisans (at a much higher level generally than Africans), and 21 per cent clerks. Previously, nearly all the Euro-peans were public servants or business executives, but they were now out-numbered substantially by engineers, technicians and artisans (*ibid.*).

This meant that since the upper strata of industry were mostly filled by Europeans and the middle strata by Asians, most Africans were under European or Asian supervisors. Although there was considerable pressure – in the form of official policy – on employers to substitute Africans for Asians wherever possible, the Africans were most suspicious of any change proposed for them. It was between Africans and Asians, however, that tension was strongest and whereas the African responded fairly readily to the orders of Europeans, his attitude to an Asian supervisor was different. The latter was alleged not only to refrain from imparting skills to Africans, but deliberately to block their advancement. In addition to being mistrusted, the Asian's position was compromised by his known liability to be overruled, in the last resort, by a European. Having, furthermore, less prestige than Europeans, he had to be more vehement than the latter to achieve results from the Africans under him. But the greatest cause of the Asian's unpopularity in the African's eyes was his obvious anxiety to show he was superior and to dissociate himself from them (*ibid.*; see also Banton, 1967, pp. 242–5).

In the course of his analysis, Sofer argues that instances of fric-tion in the cases under study do not arise only or unduly from cultural differences between the racial groups, but that 'they stem also, and perhaps more importantly, from the structure of characteristic relationships which exist between the groups' (1954, p. 72). This is a relevant observation which has the greater interest for us here because the structure specifically studied was one result-ing directly from conditions of industrialization and urbanization. Furthermore, Sofer's analysis shows how, under these same condi-tions, the Asian group became a scapegoat for African discontents – a situation which has been brought finally to a head by General Amin's recent expulsion of them for what would appear to be mainly political reasons.

Although they are an even smaller minority, the Lebanese[41] in West Africa have also played a part in urbanization and constitute another ethnically distinctive immigrant group. Nowadays, at the top level of society it is quite common for well-to-do Lebanese as well as East African Indians to meet and mix socially with Africans and members of other races, but the Lebanese origins were humble. Unlike the Indian communities concerned, the first Lebanese to arrive in Africa were from poor families among whom emigration overseas was a traditional practice, especially to the United States (Winder, 1961–2; Hanna, 1958). A combination of circumstances, including easier access and the less expensive fare, diverted part of the latter stream to Guinea, Sierra Leone and the other West African countries (Hanna, 1958).

This was at the end of the last century and at the start these almost penniless and illiterate migrants merely peddled bazaar items, such as coral beads,[42] at the street corners of Conakry, Freetown and the other coastal towns where they landed. Then, with the small profits made they bought textiles for trading upcountry where they settled, sharing the same simple conditions as the tribal Africans whose produce they purchased for resale to commercial firms on the coast. Stopping places on the railway being a convenient location for transactions of this kind,[43] the presence there of one or two such 'Syrian' stores was an important factor in the subsequent development of the villages concerned into small towns. The fact that these little settlements were thus made entrepôts for trade explains, in large measure, the present distribution and density of the Lebanese in urban terms.[44]

News of this fresh economic outlet for needy Lebanese naturally travelled back and attracted fresh immigrants. Many of these were relatives and friends of the original settlers and their arrival laid, in turn, an important basis for Lebanese prosperity as a whole because it often established a network of family ties connecting the upcountry traders with each other and with their own people on the coast (Winder, 1961–2, pp. 160–1).[45] This enabled the interchange of manufactured goods and crops grown for export to be conducted on mutually more favourable terms than could be obtained by dealing with European or African merchants. There were other advantages, too, that the Lebanese trader enjoyed over both the latter.

For one thing, accepting a lower living standard than Europeans and having members of his own family working for him he was able to conduct his business at less cost. For another, living in closer contact with his African customers he had more knowledge of them and so could grant credit with less risk than the European. African rivals the Lebanese was able to undercut by working harder and being willing to accept a smaller profit (Winder, *passim*; Stanley, 1970, p. 161). He was also in a better position to expand his business because, although the banks (all European) were most reluctant to lend to the Africans, they readily provided the Lebanese with credit (Winder, 1961–2, pp. 309–10). The upshot was that whereas Africans continued to play their role mainly as middlemen, the Lebanese acquired a share of the wholesale market, supplying Africans as well as other Lebanese with the supplies they needed as retailers.[46]

Nor has Lebanese economic activity been restricted to commerce. In Kano alone, for example, it was reported in 1957 that Lebanese had in their hands industrial enterprises which included a piggery, a shoe factory, a soap factory, a long-haul tanker and other truck business,[47] a cement block and tile factory, a kitchen-ware plant and especially peanut-crushing enterprises. Industries established in other West African areas included furniture, garment, metal assembly, transport, sawing, sweets and cakes, soft drinks, luggage, ice, perfume, ivory, cosmetics, mineral water and cigarettes. Also, not only are Lebanese stores and the residential accommodation behind or above them family-owned, but in some cities and in many 'bush' villages a large percentage of all commercial real estate and housing units have been built and owned by Lebanese. Lebanese have also acquired plantations and last, but not least, are marketers of precious stones (Winder, *op. cit.*, p. 311). This role is particularly significant in Sierra Leone which exports several million pounds worth of diamonds each year, plus an undetermined amount removed illegally (Stanley, 1970).

The obvious effect of all this enterprise and entrepreneurship is that the Lebanese control a disproportionate amount of business activity in the West African countries. This is the most important factor in the African-Lebanese relations. Like the East African Indians the Lebanese have played a conspicuous part in development but, there being already in the coastal West African towns a small but relatively well-to-do community of African professionals and merchants, there was no niche for a fresh and alien 'middle class'. Unlike the Indians, therefore, the Lebanese have never had an acknowledged position, and whereas in East Africa Indian technical assistance helped to open up the country, in West Africa European commercial firms were already well established and did not welcome newcomers except as purchasers of their own imports and sometimes as middlemen.

What perhaps is even more important in this regard is that the European administrator himself usually looked upon the Lebanese with suspicion and scarcely concealed disfavour. True, to the extent that the Lebanese were useful in various small ways such as providing goods in short supply, he was prepared to tolerate their enterprise. However, the official view was that although their industrious habits set the African a good example, Lebanese settlement was at best a necessary evil.[48] Their commercial success was put down not only to hard work but to judicious use of bribery.[49] In other words, in European eyes the Lebanese had a role somewhat analogous to that of the Jew in other contexts.[50] They were obviously culturally as well as racially different from Africans, but in some respects even less socially acceptable as equals.

Not unnaturally, this attitude had an effect, in turn, upon African estimations of the Lebanese, who did not make their position any easier by holding themselves aloof from family ties. Thus, although the first Lebanese immigrants arriving as 'bachelors' took Africans as wives or concubines, mixed unions subsequently met with strong resistance and in Jos (Nigeria), for example, two Lebanese who married African women found themselves ostracized by their own people (Winder, p. 321). Even girls of mixed parentage have been forced by their Lebanese fathers to give up the African young men they wished to marry. Also, the Lebanese preserve their separate identity, partially at least, in religion. This applies particularly to the Maronites who have several churches; but even Lebanese Moslems seem by and large to make merely token gestures to their African co-religionists. Arabic, moreover, is still the major medium of expression within the Lebanese community and, according to Winder, one particular usage in Arabic has become a focal point for African hostility to the Lebanese. This is the word '*abd* (pl. '*abid*), used traditionally to designate Africans. Basically, the word means 'servant', especially 'of God'. Since, however, it has the secondary meaning 'slave' and, by extension, the meaning 'Negro', this has not unnaturally made the word '*abd*/'*abid* a rallying point for anti-

71

F

Lebanese feelings in terms such as those of an editorial in President Nkrumah's *Evening News*: [51]

> 'Abid' is a damnable usage capable of diffusing bitterness in the most convivial society. We understand that it is principally the Lebanese (*who are feeding exuberantly fat on our hospitality* – my italics) who daily employ this insult on Africans. And Government must not hesitate to reassert the African personality in a vigorous way – that is, by promptly deporting any of these self-made demi-gods – .
>
> We are free in our country. Tell the local Lebanese traders that we are not prepared to tolerate racial insults. He who sees a free man and calls him 'slave' is less than a commodity in the old slave society – he is a brute – simple, a being whose adulterated brains have been eaten up either by excessive money grabbing tricks or merciless greed.

Establishment of social distance between themselves and West Africans has been, as explained, largely the Lebanese's own choice. At the same time, they have taken part, of course, in many aspects of community life. They have contributed very substantially to local philanthropic causes and sometimes – unwisely – to political ones.[52] They have also participated quite extensively in sport, including membership of some national teams, and have been keen supporters of horse-racing.[53] But possibly the strongest recommendation in African eyes is the Lebanese ability to acquire and willingness to use the local language.[54] In fact, in Winder's opinion, the Lebanese undoubtedly comprise the world's greatest pool of non-Africans who know West African languages (1961–2, p. 322).

Despite all this, it is likely that the Lebanese in West Africa face a future that is no less difficult and uncertain than that of the East African Indians. For, indeterminate as the Lebanese status was during the colonial era, they nevertheless had during those times a great power which was responsible ultimately for their diplomatic protection. For example, when Lebanese immigrants in Liberia complained about discrimination, France protested against it before the League of Nations in 1928, and the practice was stopped. A previous problem of nationality, when the immigrants were Ottoman subjects, was dealt with in the treaty of Lausanne, which enabled them to opt for the country of their origin, i.e. Lebanon or Syria (Winder, p. 324, (fn.)). Now, however, with African politicians in charge but frequently clashing with each other, the danger of the Lebanese being used as a pawn in these struggles for power or being made a scapegoat is even greater than in colonial times. For example, during the strikes and riots in the wake of Nkrumah's declaration of 'Positive Action', Lebanese as well as British nationals were recruited as special constables and given truncheons to help the authorities restore order. Yet, not only was it mostly the Lebanese and Syrian shops that were wrecked but there was a connection, according to Bauer, between the rioting and the official dislike of the Lebanese (Bauer, 1954, p. 83 quoted by Winder, pp. 326–7).[55]

It may be that time has ameliorated African antagonisms as strong as these but doubtful if the aftermath of Independence has produced much desire for the 'integration' of groups such as the Lebanese. Rather is the trend in the opposite direction because, as in Uganda, political and economic difficulties have put pressure on most of the African governments to safeguard the interests of their own nationals *vis-à-vis* 'foreigners'. Indeed, the term 'expatriate' has been extended beyond its original European connotation to include even fellow Africans who, when unable to prove their citizenship of the particular country, are now often debarred from employment by legislation such as the *Non-Citizens Trade and Business Act of August 20, 1969* (No. 9) in Sierra Leone. This prohibits non-citizens in general from opening new businesses or retail trade without the prior approval of the appropriate Minister in writing, but the nationality of the Lebanese being ambiguous[56] it would appear that this enactment is aimed specifically at them and with a view, hopefully, to cutting back their economic power (Stanley, 1970).

Previously, the Lebanese themselves often used to speak of their being the 'hyphen' between the Africans and the Europeans (Winder, p. 297). Now, in the above circumstances and unless West African nationalism takes a more moderate and temperate course, the Lebanese may be deprived of even a hyphenated role. Their future, in other words, may be mainly decided by the way in which nationality laws and immigration regulations are reviewed by their 'hosts'. This, in turn, will probably depend largely upon how political and diplomatic relationships develop between the various West African governments and the varying interests of the Arab world in general as well as the Lebanon itself.

73

6

Urban social organization

We have been at pains to stress that the pluralistic nature of the African 'modern' town's social structure involves a good deal of latent hostility on the part of the ethnic and tribal groups concerned, which is apt, on occasion, to break out into open conflict. True, there are law enforcement agencies, including sometimes a system of tribal administration under the jurisdiction of men approved by the tribal groups themselves. These courts deal with a number of minor offences and, as in Freetown, these 'Tribal Rulers' act as intermediaries between their own people and the municipal authority to whom the courts over which they preside are held responsible.[1] In addition, of course, there are magistrates' courts and other modern tribunals to punish other and more serious crimes which the police bring to attention. But as a means of maintaining public order, the latter body is small in size and untrained in methods of detection and has frequently to deal with people whose language the policeman does not understand. Moreover, as in all societies, the maintenance of law and order depends, in the last analysis, upon a high degree of public consensus as to what constitutes 'right' and 'wrong' behaviour.

This raises the question of migrants bringing with them to the town not only separate habits and customs but their own ideas of justice. How is any kind of social control established when these tribesmen from upcountry villages do not necessarily abandon their traditional culture? Tribal attitudes are naturally particularistic, and so what makes a possible framework of social interaction elastic enough to accommodate so much variety?

These matters have been studied within the context of the Zambian Copper Belt which is typical of new urban agglomerations in general. In other words, it has an ethnically mixed African population showing a concomitant diversity of culture which is expressed in the wide range of languages spoken, in the distinctive and sometimes exotic modes of dress and different tribal groups, and in differences in manner and behaviour. In addition, Copper Belt populations usually are highly mobile. There is a constant coming and going of people; individuals also move from one part of the town to another, and there is a characteristic absence of any single large-scale organization. Yet, despite the 'atomistic' appearance of social life and the apparent confusion of the urban scene, it is equally clear that the Africans living in these towns do not compose a mere aggregation of individuals or a disorganized rabble. The towns themselves serve certain specialized functions,[2] around which have been built complex economic and administrative institutions sufficient to ensure that the tasks necessary to them are, in the main, effectively carried out. These administrative and economic arrangements on their own introduce at least a minimum of social order and the Africans have also elaborated an intricate organization of social relationships among themselves. This system of interaction enables the mine-workers concerned to adapt to the tribal heterogeneity of their urban situation simply by fixing their fellow Africans in a given category. Categorization is based on two interrelated factors: geographical distance and cultural similarity, and it means that wide diversity of tribes is placed under a general rubric, such as Ngoni, Lozi, etc. In this way, from the point of view of the individual, all tribes other than those from his particular home area tend to be reduced into three or four categories bearing the label of those tribes who, at the coming of the Europeans, were the most powerful and dominant in the region. In other words, the tendency is for the Bemba and other tribes from the Northern Province to consider the Chewa, Nsenga, Kunda and other people from the Eastern Province, for example, as 'Ngoni'; and all tribes from Nyasaland, though they are different, as 'Nyasa' (Mitchell, 1956, *passim*).[3]

The effect of this classification, apparently, is to facilitate social relationships between strangers. This happens especially where, according to Mitchell, joking relationships existed between certain tribes, and he cites the following incident in illustration. A Bemba-speaking man grew some carrots near his house. His neighbour's children came one day and uprooted some and started to eat them.

When the Bemba-speaking man complained to his neighbour about the children's behaviour the neighbour, who spoke Nyanja, retorted in such a way that he was treating the incident as part of the Ngoni-Bemba joking relationship. The Bemba-speaking man was in fact tribally a Lungu, not a Bemba, and the Nyanja-speaking man was a Chewa. Neither of these tribes has a joking relationship with each other. The two neighbours were able to rationalize their relationship and avoid conflict by invoking the Ngoni-Bemba joking relationship (Mitchell, 1956, pp. 28–41).

The process described is one by which superficial relationships between people are determined by certain major categories within which no distinctions are recognized; but another aspect of the informal social organization is equally striking. This is the apparent ease with which, despite the continuous coming and going of people, strangers in the town are able to discover their friends and kinsfolk, or husbands and wives to trace their deserting spouses.

The explanation is, according to Epstein (1961, pp. 29–62), that each individual African is involved in a network of social ties which ramify throughout the urban community and extend both to other towns and to the tribal areas. This means, following Barnes (1954, p. 43), that each such person:

is, as it were, in touch with a number of other people some of whom are directly in touch with each other and some of whom are not. Similarly each person has a number of friends, and these friends have their own friends; some of any person's friends know each other, others do not.

In this way the organizational basis provided for social action in general is as relevant for a 'modern' African town as for the community in Norway studied by Barnes. Epstein has illustrated this in the context of Ndola, a town characteristic of the Copper Belt in general. His observations are based on the movements of one of his informants, Chanda, during a typical afternoon and evening, and since a great deal of Ndola's social life is based on the kind of social networks described, Epstein's report (1961) is quoted *in extenso*:

It was shortly after noon when Chanda[4] left off work. He decided to do a little shopping in town before returning to his house in Kabushi Suburb. On the way to town, just by the African Hospital, he met a woman who had just arrived in Ndola on the bus from Fort Rosebery. She was of his own tribe, a Lunda of Kazembe, and he greeted her. At first she did not recognize him, for it was a long time since they had last met when Chanda was on a short visit to his rural home. He introduced himself as ShiChomba, father of Chomba, and said that he was the former husband of Agnes K of Mulundu. At length the woman realized who he was and apologized for having forgotten him. 'Now I remember you well', she said, 'because your daughter resembles you so much. . . .'

After some further conversation, in which they exchanged news of friends and acquaintances, Chanda bade the woman farewell and set off again on his bicycle. Near the Government Offices (the 'Boma') he ran into his friend Thompson. Thompson was employed by the Municipality as an African Health Assistant. He was one of a small group of African assistants whose duty it was to maintain regular inspection of the location and ensure that people there adhered to the standards of hygiene laid down by the European authorities. Thompson at this time was having an extra-marital affair with a girl called Paula who was Chanda's classificatory sister. As they greeted one another a co-worker of Thompson called out from behind to ask if he were going home, but Thompson replied that he had met his 'brother-in-law' who could persuade his girl friend to be nice to him. 'You have to keep in with your brother-in-law if you are to have a good "friend" ', he added. Thompson accompanied Chanda to a store where the latter bought a broom, and then they rode off together in the direction of the location. . . .

At one of the main road junctions they found many African cyclists heading for the location. They had just knocked off and were rushing for lunch. Thompson remarked: 'Mulamo, better get off the road with these people riding crazily like this. You know, Mulamo, they are running for lunch and then come back very soon. Some are allowed only thirty minutes and will be back at two o'clock – but people like ourselves, we get home without having to sweat. Then we have a wash and rest awhile before eating – but not they. They will just eat quickly as soon as they arrive, and I am afraid that some won't even find their wives at home. This time women like going out for charcoal and firewood in the bush. These poor fellows sweat very much. . . .

There are some who don't even get home for lunch. They leave their houses very early at 5.30 in the morning and don't see their wives and children again until late in the evening. They have no bicycles – I wonder why they can't one day stop drinking beer and start saving money to buy a bicycle. . . . Their wives commit adultery very much during the day. You know, Mulamo, their wives cook *bwali* [the traditional Bemba dish of porridge with chicken relish] and take it to their boy-friends while their husbands die of hunger. Ah, well, let them suffer: it is their turn now for when we were going to school they thought we were wasting our time, and laughed at us. . . .'

At length they reached the location. Then, near the market-place in Kabushi Suburb, someone called out to Thompson, using the appropriate greeting for a man seen returning from work. They stopped and Thompson spoke to the man, whom Chanda did not know. The stranger told Thompson that his father had had to leave his job at the mine at Luanshya because he was no longer considered fit to work. As they parted and went on their way Thompson remarked: 'You know, it is as though those who have stayed in the villages would bewitch us because we no longer visit them. Let's go Chanda, that man is a real lichona.'⁵ They approached the Bottle Store where Thompson noticed a Southern Rhodesian girl passing by. 'She's an Ndebele', he said. 'If you want I'll call her so that you can "play" her.' 'But she does not know me, and anyway I don't speak Ndebele so how shall I coax her?' Chanda enquired. 'You know I've been in Bulawayo, and I know how to approach them: they're easy-going people', Thompson replied. 'Moreover, you look very smart, Mulamo, she wouldn't deny you.' But Chanda seemed unconvinced. He reminded Thompson that only recently the latter had jokingly threatened to expose one of Chanda's own peccadilloes. 'And is that Ndebele not also a woman?' he asked. 'No,' said Thompson, 'because she is not related to me, nor is she your tribeswoman. Such women are our "ration" here in town.' The two men parted and agreed to meet later in the day. . . .

When he reached his house he found that he had visitors. His wife's grandmother Ella had just arrived from Fort Rosebery. With her on this occasion was her younger sister Rose, and Alice, the elder sister of his wife, both of whom were also

living in Kabushi Suburb. Although she was a grandmother,
Ella still looked very young and, indeed, prided herself on her
youthful appearance: she regarded herself as a 'modern' woman
and was still working as a nurse at the Fort Rosebery Hospital.
She began to tell Chanda how when Laura, his wife, was a girl
she had paid for her schooling. She had hoped that Laura
would not marry early, but would continue her education at
a school in Southern Rhodesia. But then when Laura was
in Lusaka her mother had forced her into marriage with some
Lala fellow whom she didn't love. When next she went to
Lusaka, Ella continued, and saw Laura's mother she was going
to tell her something . . . and not even to write a letter all the
time! While they were talking there was a knock at the door
and Chanda's sister Anne, who was on a visit from Elizabethville
in the Belgian Congo, came in. Chanda made the introductions,
and began to explain something of his family tree. Ella soon
interrupted him: 'Do you know, ShiChomba, that this is your
own grandchild you have married?' She went into a lengthy
account of the way they were all related, and finally concluded:
'You machona, you never bother to write letters to those who
remain in the village. One day when you go there you will find
yourselves lost for those you left behind will already have gone.'
They all laughed and agreed it was so. 'But time is short,
grandmother.' Laura went and prepared food for the guests.
Chanda sat apart and read the newspaper.

In the above account Epstein distinguishes between the persons
around Chanda. There are those with whom he has close ties and
who are also more closely knit together than others; and those with
whom his ties are more or less close, but whom he sees less
frequently and who are strangers or have only tenuous links
amongst themselves. The first group, Epstein suggests, form
Chanda's *effective* network: the remainder constitute the *extended*
network and these concepts, Epstein argues, may have considerable
relevance to the discussion of problems arising within the urban
field. There is, for example, the question of social control, because
when we follow a young man like Chanda through the various links,
what we observe are a number of individuals conversing together,
recounting experiences, exchanging news of acquaintances and
friends, discussing personal matters or ideas and so on. Implicit in

much of this conversation are the norms, values and attitudes of general or special application, recognized in the society. An important part of such conversation is made up of gossip, and it is within the effective network that gossip is most intense, and the marriages, affaires, and conjugal relations of those within the effective network are among its major themes. Epstein writes (1961):

> In this way continuous gossip leads not merely to the reaffirmation of established norms, but also to the clarification and formulation of new ones. When we recall, too, the importance that attaches to prestige in this society, so that breach of the norm is also likely to involve loss of esteem in the eyes of neighbours and friends, the importance that the network may assume as an instrument of social control readily becomes apparent. Given, too, this emphasis on prestige, the ensuing struggle to which it gives rise must be expressed in the continuous adoption of new norms and patterns of behaviour, for only in this way can those who already possess high prestige ward off the challenge of their competitors. I suggest that new norms and standards of behaviour will tend to arise more frequently within the *effective* network of those who rank high on the prestige continuum, and that through the *extended* network they gradually filter down and percolate throughout the society. From this point of view the network would also appear to have importance as an instrument in examining the process of social and cultural change.

Networks in the 'modern' African town may also have a more specific basis. This has been shown by Gutkind who distinguishes between two different but overlapping types which he describes respectively as kin- and association-based. Association-based networks may or may not be linked to common tribal background, and Gutkind provides as an example of a non-tribal network the beer bars he studied in Mulago, a suburb of Kampala. Each such bar may be filled with five to twenty-five people and on a really crowded day there may be many more outside in the courtyard. On such occasions men and women of every tribe represented in the parish will sit together and jostle and joke with one another. Friends made at work or in Mulago will frequent the bar as a group. Men and women discuss the affairs and personalities of the parish, and newcomers use the occasion to make contacts, to seek lodgings and jobs. As the afternoon and evening wear on, the excitement and commotion heightens. Minor fights and bottle smashing occur and casual contacts and friendships made earlier will dissolve in anger, accusations and sudden violence. Yet, although property may be smashed, heads broken, and tribal feelings expressed bitterly, when it is all over the same people will return the next day and the next weekend, seeking companionship and friends (Gutkind, 1965, pp. 54–5).

Like the social organization described by Epstein, associationally based networks are not only very informal, they can best be isolated by means of following the activities of specific individuals rather than by tracing collective activities. Rather than providing the individual with a set of clearly defined relationships which have predictability and regularity over time, they cater merely for immediate and short-range needs (*ibid.*).

Kin-based networks, on the other hand, only come into being when either mobility is low or when circumstances favour their establishment, despite rural-urban mobility. Gutkind cites as an example of the latter Ganda residents of Mulago, the vast majority of whom move frequently and easily in and out of the parish. For instance, 31 per cent visited their kin and friends from once to five times per month; 36 per cent up to eight times every two months and 33 per cent between two and eight times every three months. Not only was this in strong contrast with non-Ganda migrants, but a Ganda resident in Mulago frequently had a steady stream of kin and friends visiting and staying with him for a few days or weeks. Such visitors would expect hospitality which involved the host in considerable extra expenditure and it was also very common for a parish resident, following his own visit home, to take back with him a youngster, perhaps his brother's child, to look after for a short or prolonged time (*ibid.*).

Consequently, although a Ganda lives away from his rural home, he is never far away from its influence, and Gutkind's conclusion is that Ganda society in Mulago rests on kin-based networks. In this regard, therefore, although the outlook of Ganda is much more 'modern', there is a similarity with the position of such ethnically and rurally bound groups as the 'Red' Xhosa.

However, it is not the general rule, either in Kampala as a whole or in other modern towns, for domestic organization itself to be based on kinship. Rather, it appears, are urban households formed in response to the *individual* requirements of men and women for economic support, companionship, sexual satisfaction and even social prestige.[6] The last mentioned factor is important mainly among educated young men and women aspiring to wed in church and so to enter into a monogamous type of union. In such cases the marriage partner is often personally chosen, but traditional obligations generally continue to affect and often disrupt the spouses' relationship. This happens because, as a result of their upbringing and the constant pressure of kinsfolk, many such husbands and wives have divided loyalties. For example, despite a man's desire to spend his available resources on the education of his own children, he may also feel it necessary for satisfactory lineage relations to see that his nephews and nieces receive a good schooling as well. A fifth of a husband's income may be spent in this way, in addition to remittances made to his mother and other maternal relatives.[7] The wife, too, will spend money on presents for her brothers and sisters and for her mother when the available cash could have been used to provide her own children with clothes or to decorate the home.

Again, rather than offend his lineage's sense of propriety, the husband may insist on his wife making customary obeisances to female relatives, younger and much less educated than herself. Furthermore, although the latter may, like many educated girls today, have married 'out of love', her hopes of a companionate relationship with her husband may be deliberately frustrated by her in-laws. They, instead of advocating fidelity, are more likely for purposes of procreation to encourage than to condemn his relations with other women. This may happen when conservative, senior kinsfolk, particularly the man's mother, resent the wife as an interloper who is seducing the boy from them. If she proves unsatisfactory in any way they seize on this avidly in order to try and prejudice the husband against her. If her fault lies in her infidelity they may 'marry' a young girl for him by customary law, paying the bridewealth and installing her in another house. Traditional attitudes are also on the husband's side, even if he has not put aside former wives married according to customary law. This, if he is now married by statute, may make him guilty of bigamy in the eyes of the law, but he is not regarded as culpable by popular opinion. Nor may there be any public objection to a husband having an irregular union with a single woman who in some countries is known as his 'outside' wife. To add to a wife's chagrin and disillusion there are also numbers of pleasure-loving women-about-town who offer, quite often, more sophisticated company than the ordinary wife, as well as sexual experience. One such union is the type contracted with *femmes libres* who, in some of the Francophone countries, enjoy so much prestige as fashionable courtesans that they can afford to pick and choose among their *coterie* of wealthy admirers.[8]

The result of these and other circumstances is that successful and durable marriages tend, in many towns, to be the exception rather than the rule. They do not necessarily end in the courts but often involve a disharmonious relationship between the spouses. This applies to households which are, in fact, based upon male and female partners who are husband and wife in the legal meaning of these words. True, in the élite groups of leading politicians, well-known professional men and churchmen and for the completely traditional sections, marriages must be correctly performed under one or other system of law. However, as in Kampala for example, many urban households fit into neither system and so it is convenient sometimes to make a somewhat arbitrary distinction between 'permanent' (or 'real') and temporary wives. A permanent wife is one who has married according to tribal custom in the rural district, one who has undergone a Christian or Moslem ritual, or one who is partner to a civil or District Registrar marriage. These three forms of marriage may be accompanied by a transaction of bridewealth. There is a fourth category also, involving women who are partners to some intra- and intertribal unions established in town, in which bridewealth may have been paid and/or children previously or subsequently born. A temporary wife is usually one who has been secured in town by a man to satisfy his domestic and sexual needs. No bridewealth will have been paid for her. Normally, she will be childless, but occasionally a man may impregnate his temporary wife; then both partners, and eventually also neighbours, may begin to regard the union as permanent, with at least the stated expectation that the union will be continued at one spouse's rural home when the period of urban employment ceases (Parkin, 1966a).

In fact, in Kampala the bulk of the population contract tribal marriages which, however, often lack certain traditional essentials. For example, as a result of migration, important relatives are frequently absent, and the wife may not have been introduced to her husband's people. But tribal marriages are considered 'good' marriages, which are more 'convenient' than a Christian marriage. It is held that if a woman does not meet the expected standards, such as being able to cook and to have children, or if she is unfaithful to her husband, he can, in a tribal marriage, 'return her' to her father and get his money back. It is also argued that tribal marriage, like free marriage, is less filled with tension 'because in a Christian marriage you must live according to religion', and also in a tribal marriage 'we do things we have been told to by our grandfathers'. However, these objections to Christian marriages are often not meant to be taken very seriously, for when informants are questioned closely about the kind of marriage they would like their sons and daughters to have, the answer is almost always that Christian marriage is preferred (Southall and Gutkind, 1957, pp. 53–7).

Legally speaking, therefore, it is necessary to be clear about the way in which the parties concerned go about the matter. Is a customary procedure followed or are arrangements made individually? The latter are from the indigenous point of view merely extra-marital unions with lovers, and in Monrovia, for instance, it appears to be traditionally acceptable for either a married or a single man to keep such a 'friend' or *megi* (Fraenkel, 1964, pp. 113–14). 'Friendship', in these terms, is a temporary affair and it is frequently entered into to meet an expediency. If, for example, a marriage breaks up, economic reasons may make it imperative for the man to seek another partner, and for the woman to do so also. The man may find himself with a number of children. If he cannot make arrangements to live with his parents' family, he must find a woman to keep house for him. The woman may also find herself with the smaller children and without adequate support (Little, 1973a).

Like the above *megi* relationship, free marriages combine the advantages of a more or less settled existence of being looked after by a man, with the freedom to leave his house at any time. There is also a certain seal of respectability, and a further advantage is that there is apparently less feeling of tension than in a more casual affair. As a Ganda informant put it: 'You can be sure that your wife is at home when you come back from work', and also of importance to many of the men is the fact that in a free marriage the women may agree to have children (Southall and Gutkind, 1957). One of

the greatest advantages of this kind of sexual contact is the willingness of the community to recognize it. It provides both parties with
the opportunity of trying out a spouse before they settle down and
have a 'real' marriage. This is important because (quoted in
Southall and Gutkind, 1957, pp. 165–6):

> If you take the first woman you find in a bar or on the street
> you may not get the right woman. She may not be educated and
> perhaps she does not want to obey. I think that all women
> should do what their husbands want. A woman may want to
> have a Christian marriage, but the husband does not want to
> spend all that money. Some men want to have a tribal marriage
> because they can send the woman back to her father and get
> their money back if they find that she cannot cook, cultivate
> food, or if she lives with other men.

Furthermore, although the majority of urban households consist
of five, six, or seven people, a proportion are constituted of single
men. In Freetown, for example, forty-one households out of 268
were of this type (Banton, 1957), while in Jinja, Sofer and Sofer
(1955) found that the majority of their sample of households were
males living alone (48 per cent). In Jinja the Luo bring their wives,
probably because they contemplate a longer period of residence
than other tribes, but the practice of leaving wives and children
behind is much more common. This situation, together with the fact
that some send their children to the country to be educated,
accounts for the 75 per cent of the Sofers' sample who had no
children. A few households, on the other hand, consist of men
without wives but with children, some of whom are married; either
they have no wives or the latter are back in the village for the
delivery of a child and during the nursing period (Izzett, 1961, p.
307). Also, the head of the household may at times be a woman and
there are several variants of matricentred households. For example,
one finds quite frequently 'outside wives', divorcees, widows,
femmes libres, or prostitutes living with relatives, their children or
lovers.[9]

Most of the above domestic groupings contain at least one bread-
winner, but opportunities of well-paid and regular employment are
confined mainly to the educated class and to skilled workers who
together form a relatively small proportion of the town's population. Moreover, few, if any, of the modern welfare state's safeguards

are available. Apart from the civil service, such pension schemes as exist for older people or to cover sickness or disability are at the embryonic stage,[10] and there is little national assistance to provide for the destitute or the unemployed. True, the wealthier families described are generally in a position to look after poorer relatives as well as their own members, but for the reasons given domestic life among them as well as among the large immigrant section tends to lack a stable foundation. Its absence is the more significant because most of the latter people came directly from a kinship organization which, in addition to mutual aid, supplied the individual with moral support and even catered for his religious needs.

The last mentioned point brings us directly to various new cults which combine elements of Christianity and Islam with traditional beliefs. One of these groups – Blekete in eastern Ghana – claims to cure illness and other disorders by supernatural power or vodu. Blekete has rules which prohibit the eating of pork and the wearing of shoes in the Blekete 'temple'. Other injunctions are similar to the Ten Commandments of the Old Testament and, on the cultural level, the use of kola nuts, the 'toga' worn by the Blekete priest, and some of the percussion instruments used are of northern Ghanaian extraction. Local observances, in turn, are expressed in warnings against indiscreet sex relations and the return of bridewealth. Further, the form and structure of Blekete priesthood itself is substantially identical to indigenous practice (Fiawoo, 1959).

A slightly different form of cult, though concerned specifically with 'witch-finding', also deals with securing jobs, economic gain, or protection while travelling. There is a priest attended by four priestesses, and anyone can become a member, or a member of the 'fetish', by paying a small sum, taking a ritual bite or two of kola, and undertaking to obey the fetish rules which are similar to those of Blekete. Not only those who fear witches join the cult, for many members regard it as an insurance against any danger, including not only the so-called pagan but also the literates, Christian and Moslem alike (Christensen, 1962, p. 277).

These syncretist cults attract many devotees, largely because they claim to cope with and resolve individual and social problems peculiar to the urban environment apparently beyond the scope of traditional ritual. These are frequently, for example, acts of physical violence, robbery and petty larceny, drunkenness and prostitution (Busia, 1950, pp. 84–114). There are also various illnesses, such as venereal disease, which cause sterility and melancholia as well as physical discomfort. These new maladies and disorders of society are very much more common in the town than in the countryside, and so the tendency, quite often, is for witchcraft accusations to be made on a wider scale and for there to be a greater fear of evil influences in general. Part of the explanation is the individualism and competitive spirit evoked by new forms of social relationship as well as new occupations. This is frequently rationalized in terms of personal fortune or misfortune having a supernatural connection. A farmer growing cocoa for cash, for example, may lose his entire crop through blight; a clerk may be dismissed from his post in an office; or a girl's lover may be attracted by another woman, but the cause is rationalized as malevolent forces being at work, or jealous and unscrupulous rivals possessing a medicine more powerful than one's own (Little, 1965, pp. 91–3).

Various neo-Christian prophetic or messianic movements attract adherents for similar reasons. One of the most notable was named after William Wade Harris, a Grebo by origin, who was born in Liberia. He travelled through what was then French West Africa and the Gold Coast preaching against fetish, lying, strong drink and adultery. After Harris's death the cult dwindled, but it later revived and became widespread in the Ivory Coast, particularly Abidjan. Baptism and funeral rites were its most important rituals. Numerous other prophetic cults included that of Deima, founded by a Godi woman. The prophetess, who had been baptized a Protestant, had an encounter with a serpent through whom she acquired ashes and water endowed with miraculous power of protecting believers from all diseases. Devotees could obtain a supply of this medicine for a few francs, but if they harboured any bitterness in their hearts while drinking it they might fall ill or even die. Membership of the cult itself was open to anyone prepared to renounce his present religion and to swear not to injure his neighbours by poison or sorcery (Holas, 1954).[11]

Mention should also be made of the numerous heterogeneous 'church' groups which had developed a type of worship and an ethos compounded of Christian and indigenous elements. These are sects which have split away from, or sprung up in relative independence of, the older mission churches. Some of these 'churches' model their organization on the pattern of the Protestant or Roman Catholic missions from which they have seceded, but permit polygamy. In others, emphasis is placed upon the 'prophet' or 'leader' of the sect who was called to found the church.[12] In one of these sects in Ghana, every new member is baptized by sprinkling and the laying-on of hands following his public confession of sins; he or she is then given a new 'heavenly name' by the prophet.[13]

A large number of groups, therefore, are organized specifically for the pursuit of spiritual benefit and protection in one form or another. Most voluntary associations, however, are formed to cater for their members' material needs in the shape of money. This applies particularly in commerce because the main requirement of most of the petty traders thronging the markets is capital. This brings into being a wide variety of schemes and one widely practised method is known among the Yoruba as *esusu* (Little, 1965, p. 52). *Esusu* is merely a fund to which a number of individuals make fixed contributions of money at stated intervals; the total amount contributed by the entire group being assigned to each of the members in turn. Rotating credit associations of this kind are widespread and although some fairly complicated developments of the basic pattern exist in Nigeria,[14] the arrangements in East Africa are usually simple and informal. The greatest danger, especially in urban areas, is default. It is necessary, therefore, that members should know each other well enough for there to be mutual confidence and that they should have regular cash incomes of a sufficiently similar level to minimize temptation. Consequently, the most popular form in East Africa is one constituted of employees in government and commercial offices. Organizations of this kind are said to be widespread in Nairobi where, sometimes, the members collect in a bar on pay-day. In commercial firms the amounts may be automatically deducted from salaries by the pay-clerk, who hands over the lump sum to the member whose turn it is. The motive here is to get capital for radios, repayment of debts, or for payment of hire-purchase instalments on cars (Jellicoe, 1968, pp. 54–5).

In Kampala, although similar associations are found among the wealthier Ganda shop-keepers, they also exist among the poorer sections of the community. For example, porters and medical orderlies in two hospitals put in one-quarter to one-third of their monthly wages; while in Nairobi, shoe-blacks run associations on the same daily basis as they earn money (*ibid.*).

It is also the case that mutual benefit societies in general usually have social activities in addition to their economic interests. Some Ghanaian associations, for example, include excursions and picnics; concerts, singing, dancing and drumming; religious talks and discussions, literacy classes, debates and cinema shows; first-aid services; initiation ceremonies for new members; and the laying of wreaths on graves of former members. The expense is met out of regular dues which pay for such things as rent, lighting, books, stamps, cups, forms, flags, banners, drums, messengers, tables, and in some cases honoraria to secretaries. In addition, collections are made for money required for the various forms of assistance rendered to members, and for the help which more than half the societies studied extend to the wider public, especially the socially handicapped. Members take presents in money and in kind to hospitals and prisons and to other institutions where the inmates may be in need of advice and encouragement (Acquah, 1958, pp. 87–91).

Other occupational and professional associations are concerned with the status and remuneration of their members as workers (Busia, 1950, p. 27). In Sekondi-Takoradi, for example, there are unions of carpenters, shoemakers, drivers, sugar-sellers, seamen, cooks and stewards, all of which also offer their members, as a principal benefit, the assurance of a decent burial. There are also modern crafts such as teachers, gunsmiths, tailors, and barbers, as well as certain trade unions which have come spontaneously into being. These organizations, too, frequently provide small sickness and accident benefits, and it is symptomatic of the general emphasis on mutuality that even recreational groups have similar practices. For example, in Freetown various *compins* (companies) exist in order to perform 'plays' of traditional music and dancing. The music is provided mainly by native drums, calabash rattles, and xylophones, and is accompanied by singing. The dancing, which like the music shows strong western influence, is somewhat reminiscent of English country dancing, but it varies with the *compin* concerned. A 'play' is generally given in connection with some important local event, and the general public is expected to donate money to the *compin* on these occasions. Money collected in the form of weekly subscriptions is used to help members in sickness or bereavement (Banton, 1957, pp. 171, 173).

Voluntary associations are important in this situation because they provide a link between the traditional and the urban way of life. This is particularly true of a further species of association – the ethnic or regional union – which, on the one hand, emphasizes tribal duties and obligations, and urges, on the other hand, the adoption of a modern outlook and social practices. In other words, these regional associations, as 'adaptive mechanisms', provide for the rural migrant a cultural bridge, conveying him from one kind of social universe to another.[15]

Organizations of this kind are widespread in East and West Africa, the term used in the French-speaking countries being *association d'originaire*. They are referred to in this way to distinguish them from associations that also practise mutual aid but whose members are united by other factors, such as age, occupation and education.[16] In some of these organizations, which are entirely composed of migrants, there are two or three levels, starting with clan associations. At the next level are location and sub-tribe associations, and the final level is that of the whole tribal union or association. In Kampala the Luo association is by far the most viable and is properly to be understood as a node in a network of such associations established in many towns in East Africa. This union has established schools and nurseries in addition to organizing the Luo interlocation soccer competions and occasional dances. It is the clan association, however, that deals with the more frequent and commonplace urban problems directly affecting the individual, including self-help, mutual aid, repatriation of destitute, unemployed members, etc. (Parkin, 1969, pp. 151–4).[17]

In the clan associations of Kampala, the leaders and most regular and active members are below the socio-economic average for the tribe's urban population (*ibid.*, p. 153). Speaking more generally, however, there is a mixture of social elements. In Nigeria, for example, although most members are illiterate, there are individuals of every class, including school teachers, doctors and lawyers, as well as day labourers. In Dar es Salaam the leaders are the older men (Leslie, 1963, pp. 37–43). Sometimes educated people look down upon tribal associations as parochial and backward looking. Many others, however, have taken the lead in founding and directing them, and there are occasions indeed when affiliation is considered a duty.[18] Social activities include an annual celebration, the organization of dances on festival days, and of sports and games for the young people. Persons newly arrived from the country areas or returned from overseas are welcomed, and in these ways the migrants abroad can maintain contact with their rural friends and relatives (Little, 1965, pp. 28, 29, 33, 34).

The immediate effect, therefore, of the ethnic association is to increase tribal consciousness by reminding people of their common origin. This sentiment is further strengthened by exhortations to fraternity. Members are urged actively to regard each other as brothers and sisters, with the obligation to assist and sympathize with one another in every kind of difficulty. Yet, paradoxically,[19] the fact that the regional association is often under educated leadership gives to certain of its activities at the same time a modern slant. This comes about because 'progressively' minded young men see, in resuscitation of the tribal spirit, an opportunity for building up larger structures that may, in turn, be used to bring about social change. Under this 'progressive' influence, therefore, many associations set out to improve their home town, village, or state, the idea being to provide up-to-date amenities – schools, hospitals and roads – equal to those of the place into which the migrants have moved. This is done through home branches of the association abroad. These are formed by returning members who wish to continue the comradely times they have enjoyed while away.[20]

Special attention has been given to the complex structure and modern aims of the regional (ethnic) association because of its implications for urbanization, especially in terms of 'resocialization'. For example, not only is the rural migrant brought into close personal contact with individuals of higher social status than himself, but interacting with them in an informal and social atmosphere encourages him to aspire to different habits and ways. It makes him more amenable to new standards of dress and personal hygiene, the advantage being that he is regarded no longer as a country bumpkin but is able to keep pace with 'real' townsmen (Little, 1965, p. 89). Moreover, although educated people are the associations' principal leaders, a host of minor offices and titles are generally available. These give even the most humble member an opportunity to feel that he 'matters' (Little, 1965, p. 88). They also encourage him, through co-operation with the senior officials, to develop a more broadminded attitude towards non-tribesmen. The association being conceived of as a single family, richer members habitually assist those who are less well-off by loaning money, standing sureties and using influence over jobs. This is regarded as an obligation, but it is also a way of gaining prestige.

Further, an ability to wield power and influence in the wider community may accrue from holding office in an association itself. This happened when, for example, some Nigerian unions provided the nucleus of emerging political parties, thereby enabling the leaders of the associations concerned to move naturally into posts of national importance. Somewhat similarly, according to a recent report (La Fontaine, 1970, pp. 191ff.) concerning politics in Kinshasa, tribal loyalties take the place of political ideology. This meant that among the most important pawns in the 'power game' were voluntary associations, whose organization was used, sometimes as the foundation for a political party. In other cases, parties had been formed by the alliance of leaders of a number of tribal associations. In Kampala, too, an attribute of the Luo union was its potential as a form of leadership in local politics. For example, one Luo candidate at the 1962 municipal council elections was a secretary of the union, and an appointed Luo councillor played an important part in certain of the association's activities, and frequently addressed meetings (Parkin, 1969, pp. 37, 50). A correlation was also found between leadership in the Luo community and business activity. The Luo were the only tribe other than the Ganda to own property and run businesses on any scale and a large proportion of leaders in the Luo union and in some location associations were 'businessmen'.

In these terms, therefore, the regional association can be seen as significant for urbanization in two ways. Firstly, the social organization it provides serves, by articulating with politics and business, to underpin new urban structures. Secondly, quite often its administration is designed in such a way that many of the office-holders have western titles, such as doctor and nurse; and there may be further officials, such as overseer, solicitor, lawyer, and so on. To a large extent these roles are make-believe, but the relevant thing is that their performance also involves some knowledge of urban patterns of conduct (Banton, 1957, p. 182). In addition, members may be required to sit on committees, and, as already explained, many ethnic associations advocate up-to-date amenities. They endeavour to spread 'civilization', and the fact that these ideas are propagated within a familiar context makes the innovations seem less strange. At the association's premises, a man can sit with his fellow countrymen, play and listen to traditional music, and eat traditional dishes without feeling anxious or ashamed about the ridicule of local people. Meetings themselves invariably begin with a prayer, and for every deceased member there is not only a funeral but a wake, which everybody attends. Also, not only is every meeting or celebration a reminder of home ties and obligations, but social sanctions have a customary ring. A migrant's reputation for good or evil accompanies him to the town, and within the union abroad gossip restricts behaviour as effectively as in the rural village.

Of course, other urban associations, too, discipline their members who, in some women's groups for example, are upbraided if they create strife among other women and may be expelled if they are constant troublemakers in the home. But ethnic associations seem able to exercise an even stricter control. This is shown in a Nigerian union in Freetown which decrees that no member shall take legal steps against any other member without first bringing the matter up at a meeting of the association; it also claims the right to submit evidence in court of its own judgment is ignored by the complainant (Banton, 1957, p. 190).[21]

The fact that social sanctions can be applied in this way makes the regional association the more significant for urbanization. It is able to arbitrate to this extent because it replaces the social control exercised in the rural village by neighbours, extended family, and local community. Since senior kinsmen and other traditional figures of authority are often lacking from his immediate environment, a person in trouble turns to the head of his association for help or advice. His position is similar to that of a junior member of the lineage; he is dependent on the favour and goodwill of the group's leaders. In fact, the association's practice of helping financially its own members is probably one of the main sources of control. It enables the officials concerned to exert their authority more readily, particularly since recalcitrant members are sometimes the most needy. The result is that the role of ethnic associations is not confined to supervising private conduct. In addition, they frequently have formal rules of admission[22] and regulations that are designed to govern the public behaviour of members as well as their relations with each other. For example, a member who is reported for quarrelling in the town, for abusing elderly people, or for putting curses on others will be warned to correct his behaviour. Similarly, when members are adulterous, cause disorders at meetings, or are known to steal, they may be suspended, fined or even expelled. The last mentioned penalty is, of course, the ultimate sanction and is effective because, given tribal antagonisms, migrants may often need protection. Moreover, they know that there may be little hope of companionship outside their own people.

As indicated, it is the major towns of East and West Africa and among migrant groups, in particular, that voluntary associations are mainly to be found. Yet, even in these terms, they are far from being omnipresent and the extent to which they are able to recruit members seems to be dependent on the interplay of structural factors peculiar to a given situation as well as expediency. Thus, in Freetown, for example, the two major groups of migrants are the Temne and the Mende. Dancing *compins* were widely organized and keenly supported by the Temne. The Mende, however, took little part in such activities, probably because for educational and other reasons they were already socially and occupationally at an advantage compared with all other tribal groups (Little, 1967a, *passim*).

Consequently, our conclusion is that although voluntary associations have their place in any general theory of African urbanization, the other social institutions and mechanisms mentioned are equally integral to the 'modern' town social organization. The latter, part-institutionalized and part-informal, represents an adaptation to circumstances which, in terms of cultural diversity – differences in language, customs and religion – might almost amount to Durkheim's notion of *anomie*, or 'normlessness.' Nevertheless, procedures have evolved on a basis of traditional experience which provide working systems of control and so furnish a solid enough foundation for patterns of co-operation to develop *across*, as well as *along*, ethnic lines.

It is for these reasons that, as indicated earlier, our approach has not been confined to urban patterns of social behaviour *per se*. In other words, given that contemporary African urbanization is peculiarly a phenomenon of urban population growth, it is to the dynamic factors underlying the latter that primary attention needs to be given.

7

Conclusions

In the foregoing pages it has been intimated that contemporary urban development results primarily from the expansion of capitalist enterprise in the African continent. We considered some aspects of the social effects and noted among other things that the population growth involved gives rise in present circumstances to two apparently contradictory processes, the one asserting ethnic factors, the other leading in the direction of 'class'. The result of this dichotomy is, as we have stressed, more marked in some cities than others because the size of the highly educated, more westernized groups tends to be variable. A further, more specific, point has also to be remembered; this is that numerous West African cities continue to contain or have on their periphery what is known in Ghana as the *zongo* and in Nigeria as the *sabon-gari* ('new town'). These places are the customary abode of African 'strangers' who in the Ghanaian and West Nigerian towns concerned are mainly Hausa and other islamicized groups, and Yoruba and Ibo in the northern towns of Nigeria. Indeed, sometimes the *zongo* has more inhabitants than the rest of the township (cf. Steel, 1961, p. 273). Further, the older European-established as well as the traditionally based cities still contain considerable 'pockets' of quasi-tribal culture in close proximity both to huge, recently erected buildings of steel and concrete[1] and the white-collared class who work in them. Where, however, residential separation has taken place on an extensive scale there are several neighbourhoods, each with its own relatively self-sufficient social life.

As implied, Ibadan tends to show this character; but Stanleyville (now Kinsangani) seemingly provides an even clearer example because, according to Pons (1969, pp. 6–8), the inhabitants of one such area will tend to be members of the same tribe, and the incidence of 'mixed' or non-tribal marriage there will be low. Local recreational activities will be organized on a largely exclusive tribal basis, although at least some *évolués* will take part in them and are also likely to mix with the illiterate section during leisure-time, casually drinking and gossiping with them. Also, in this kind of area people will talk to each other exclusively in their own tribal vernacular. In another part of the town, however, the inhabitants will mostly be heard conversing in one or both of the *linguae francae*, Swahili and Lingala (and occasionally in French). Here, members of many different tribes will live side by side and commonly share the same dwelling compounds, and the incidence of non-tribal marriage will be high. Also, since informal friendship groups and formal voluntary associations will often consist of members of different tribes, a measure of anti-tribal sentiment may be in evidence. People will be found ready to argue that 'tribe counts for nothing'; or that, 'unlike our fathers, we no longer look at tribe nowadays'. In other words, this neighbourhood being occupied largely by the French-speaking *évolués*, it would be characterized by quite different patterns of culture and behaviour from places where the uneducated masses of manual workers live.

A situation of this kind takes us back again to the complexities of African urban life. It makes it appropriate, therefore, to re-examine now the concept of urbanization itself and to consider how far it has helped to illuminate the sociology of urban population growth. We have seen that the latter phenomenon seems to be marked – at least in sub-Saharan terms – by the settlement of populations which are ethnically heterogeneous and relatively transient. Also, usually, adult males preponderate numerically over adult females and the younger age groups over the older; and, of course, a relatively large proportion of the population concerned depend economically upon the sale of goods, labour, or services. Since, as remarked earlier, African urban population growth seems to be characterized by these common demographic and economic features there is, perhaps, some advantage in using them as criteria. However, while also accepting Wirth's minimal definition of 'a relatively dense permanent settlement of socially heterogeneous individuals', it would be wrong necessarily to confine ourselves to western notions of urbanism alone. This reservation is important even if we postulate that most Africans in towns tend to share motivations similar to those of urbanities elsewhere – a quest for wealth, improvement of social position, economic security, etc. It needs to be made because there is, in fact, a good deal of variety in the ways in which these goals are socially symbolized. Certainly, African societies have been closely in contact with European civilization and so the long-term trend may indeed have a western *terminus ad quem*. From an empirical standpoint, however, the direction of this trend cannot be so readily predicted. Its nature is ambiguous enough to suggest that the idea of tribal societies becoming more and more westernized is not always useful or legitimate. True, something is known about both the present state of such societies and the conditions under which they are moving. But the most one can say is that it is a movement involving change of a radical order which, fundamentally, is characterized by the exchange of smaller for larger settlement patterns. This is in line with our original argument that the modern African town was brought into being principally to provide business and industry, as well as administration, with urban facilities. Yet, even a statement as general as this would be misleading if it implied that economic development is only significant within city zones and thereby kept out of sight a further essential feature of the contemporary scene.

This is the fact that not only does a very small proportion of Africa's total population inhabit towns, but in the countryside itself there has been a steady increase in the growth of crops intended for urban consumption in addition to the much larger markets overseas. Commercial activity of this kind involves the employment of wage-labour; and, coupled with intensive cultivation on plantations, it results in some agricultural centres becoming as functionally important for the market economy as the 'modern' town itself. Parts of south-eastern Nigeria provide a well-known example of this phenomenon which may exhibit many of the characteristics commonly associated with 'urban' rather than 'rural' areas. Also, in the Victoria Division of the Cameroons, over 61,000 persons among a population of 85,000 were found to be immigrants; and, when studied in 1960, this Division had as a whole almost twice as many males as females. On the plantations themselves the proportion of males was approximately 70 per cent of the population and, there being so many unattached men about, the temptation had existed for many years for indigenous women to leave or avoid married life in the villages in order to live as concubines of the immigrants or as prostitutes. Not only do 'stranger quarters' of the immigrant settlements contain numbers of these women, but they are also found in the villages themselves. The frequency of divorce, too, is high; and, according to Ardener, 63 per cent of all legitimate unions ever completed by a sample of 1,062 village women, and 40 per cent of all legitimate unions ever contracted, had ended in divorce. There were 683 divorces per 1,000 women (Ardener, 1961, pp. 93–4).[2]

But, irrespective of 'urban' phenomena of the latter sort, one should not imagine either that life in the African countryside has already been indelibly stamped with the seal of the town or that in the latter itself there is anything like the extreme individualism and anomie that some writers associate with western urbanism. For one thing, as we have stressed, even the more cosmopolitan type of city tends to have a local core of indigenous inhabitants as well as the numerous migrants who persist in following traditional ways. Moreover, not only can these groups of inhabitants be seen in respect of their socio-cultural characteristics as more 'rural' than 'urban', but the extent to which the city's population *as a whole* participates in truly modern (western) institutions is small. Only in terms of work is the proportion substantial because, despite the many voluntary associations and social clubs to which a person can belong, most such organizations are of a quasi-traditional kind and so attract mainly the less lettered people. The wider mental horizon of the educated classes, it is true, conduces towards a different orientation, including political and kindred interests, but even among them informal social gatherings tend to be on monosexual lines or largely confined to meetings of kinsfolk for ceremonies or to talk over family business.

If, then, the social institutions associated ordinarily with urban-industrial conditions actively involve such a small minority, why attach so much methodological importance to 'urbanization'? As explained earlier, 'urbanization' has been used throughout this essay for analytical purposes, and so must it suffice in the end merely to regard this concept as a descriptive way of indicating movement from something regarded as 'rural'? Or, alternatively, should we think of it basically – as some writers have suggested – in terms of commitment to urban residence?[3]

A drawback to the latter view of urbanization is that the criteria upon which the definition itself have to be based seem to involve some circularity. The real difficulties, however, lie deeper. They consist, firstly, in the fact that most social scientists, being Westerners, are accustomed to think of 'town' and 'village' as separate things when, in fact, conceptualism on these lines is not made in every culture. Indeed, ironically enough, it is especially irrelevant to the particular type of African urbanism found in the Western Sudan, where, as explained, cities are often inhabited by farmers. In these Yoruba towns, there is the *ìlù*, or nucleated settlement, but it does not stop short at the mud walls enclosing the town. It extends into the farmlands beyond, and so the *ìlù* boundaries are co-terminous, in a sense, with those of the furthest plots farmed by members of the residential unit within the clustered settlement itself. Conceptually, in other words, the Yoruba city is not distinguished from its farming hinterland; the whole complex is to be seen rather as a unit radiating out from a core consisting of the *oba* (king) and council (Krapf-Askari, 1969, pp. 25–6). As mentioned, Yoruba towns are often large in size; but in Sierra Leone, Mende settlements, though small, have a very similar pattern. This is based on a local group of kinsmen recognized under the expression *kuwui*, meaning literally 'compound'. In a limited sense, *kuwui* is simply an aggregate of individual farming households occupying a particular place; but, sociologically speaking, the Mende town and the countryside around it really form a single system of kinship. The town is made up of many separate localities containing the compounds of its inhabitants, and with each 'urban' locality is associated one or more 'rural' localities, comprising village and farmlands (Little, 1967b, pp. 101–5).[4] The Africans concerned recognize social differences between people whose residence is in the town and those residing in the 'bush'. Since, however, the inhabitants of both depend basically upon the same subsistence economy, village and town do not constitute a polarity. There is, in consequence, no real rural-urban continuum.

This is not to suggest that in traditional urbanism every such combination of town and villages was a socio-political unit on its own. In fact, West Africa's seventeenth- and eighteenth-century history is marked not only by a continuous struggle for political power between various states but by a wide network of trading relations. Hausa capital cities, for example, were centres of congregation for foreign merchants from other parts of the region as well as North Africa. In return for manufactured wares, salt, dates, and other merchandise, Hausaland provided grain, leather products, woven cloth and other manufactured goods. In addition, Hausaland and Bornu, straddling the savannah and scrubland belt south of the Sahara, occupied a middleman's position in the exchange of complementary articles between North Africa (and indirectly Europe) with the peoples of the forest belt (Ajayi and Crowder, 1971, vol. 1, pp. 520ff.). Yet, despite the process of state-formation and the state-building continuously going on, few of the competing states ever possessed power enough to impose their hegemony effectively over the others. More often than not victory in a war only resulted in the acquisition of booty, and even if the conquered became a tributary state, tribute itself was only rendered so long as the conquereor used military force to exact it (*ibid.*). Life probably went on largely as before and, extensive as their trading relations were, these cities remained economically autonomous (*ibid.*).

We stress this point because there is something to be learned from a comparison of 'traditional' and 'modern' urbanism. Instead, however, of seeking to understand the difference in terms of social, cultural, or demographic characteristics we need to look at it from the angle of 'function'. In other words, what is the city's *raison d'être*? What particular purpose or set of purposes does it serve?

Since, as we have just implied, there is apparently a close connection between city and state in traditional urbanism, the reply in this case may be quite straightforward. That is to say, although external political and other factors affected the course of events, the traditional town had a definite identity of its own. For the surrounding countryside it constituted the hub of community affairs and the more so when, as among the Yoruba, the city was the seat of the *oba*. Religion and ritual revolved mainly around him as a species of divine king and this meant that not only the *oba* was the personification of his city, but that the latter, in turn, had an essentially ceremonial and cultic role.

Parallels with this kind of function are lacking from the 'modern' town. Nor can they be expected when the latter urban settlements, unlike the traditional city, were never intended or created to serve local needs. True, numbers of the 'modern' town's inhabitants may be drawn from its own hinterland; but, as we have seen, connections with the latter are of a secondary character. This is because, having been brought into being for the benefit of outside capitalism, the 'modern' town's primary relationship is with countries abroad. As Hutchinson has put it (1968):[5]

> The first rungs of the development ladder were climbed on the exchange of African raw materials for the manufactures of overseas urban communities. There has been little development of the system of exchange between African countryside and African towns. Further, African towns have grown up very largely where they can best service the exchange between Africa and Europe or America. Consider the dominance in urban West Africa of Lagos, Tema, Accra, Takoradi and Freetown. Indeed their food supplies as well as their trade is very substantially overseas orientated.

Consequently, the principal functions that the 'modern' town performs are not intrinsic to the city itself, but originate instead in an outside, encompassing system of politico-economic relations. This, of course, is controlled not within the African country concerned but by outside forces, and its ramifications include some specialization. Trading-commercial cities are the most important in this regard, but sea and inland ports account for almost half of the urban population in the countries concerned (Nigeria and Mozambique are not counted) (Hance, 1970, pp. 262–4).[6] Such a situation of neo-colonialism, as it is called,[7] means that, although independent in theory, the state in question has its political policy directed by another power which quite often was the former ruler of that territory and with which it continues to conduct most of its trade and other business.[8] In other cases, neo-colonial control may be exercised by a consortium of financial interests which are not specifically identifiable with any particular state.[9]

The upshot is a far-reaching network of political and economic relations crossing the whole continent and stretching from 'China to Peru'. The international markets involved fluctuate and the chain-reactions thus generated extend beyond the world of industry and business. They also affect, directly or indirectly, the everyday life of virtually every individual townsman and peasant alike. For example, transactions conducted in Wall Street or the City of London over some locally produced commodity may have the effect of raising or lowering living standards among both the rural and the urban communities of the African country concerned. True, the actual production of exports and the secondary wholesale and retail distribution of consumer goods are almost totally in African hands. But the largest financial, wholesale, import-export, and manu-facturing units[10] are foreign-controlled and provide a focus around which the African-owned units revolve and into which they feed (cf. Green, 1970, p. 290). Indeed the degree of dependence on foreign finance for public sector investment runs from 100 per cent in certain extremely underdeveloped and/or tiny states such as Dahomey to 25 to 35 per cent in certain mineral boom economies, including Zambia and Gabon (*ibid.*, p. 291). Such foreign aid and investment obviously varies in nature and the employment of local labour is naturally regulated directly or indirectly by its ebb and flow.

We have laid emphasis on this secondary and even tertiary part played individually[11] by most African countries in the international politico-economic process because it is reflected, in turn, in the 'modern' town's function. This being dependent so largely upon the working of the overall system means that many such towns and urban agglomerations exist in little more than a physical sense. They barely achieve a civic personality even when, as corporations, they exercise municipal powers and thereby gain a legal and constitutional identity. It is arguable, of course, that this applies in essence also to many of the developed countries. However, although there are numerous European and North American urban areas which have been either deliberately created or come 'spontaneously' into being simply to provide dormitories for commuters or workers in nearby factories, the position in most of the developed world is quite different. Cities like Washington, Paris, Rome, London, Moscow, Peking and so on have prestige and a 'personality' of their own for historical reasons as well as being the capitals of great powers. This is coming to be true also of some cities in the independent African countries, such as Lagos, Accra and Nairobi; but, for reasons already explained, most African towns do not reliably personify urban institutions in the conventional meaning of such terms. Rather, as we stressed, do they tend simply to mirror – though in traditionally conditioned ways – what is happening outside in the world-wide operations of the exogenous forces referred to. It is the latter, in other words, which mostly determine whatever modes of standardized co-activity do eventually take root, thereby making the urbanization of tribal inhabitants a process of adaptation. These people are constrained, in effect, to fit their behaviour into, and to adjust to, the social matrix created, as Mitchell puts it, 'by the modern commercial, industrial and administrative framework' (1966).

These considerations may, it is hoped, enable the significance of contemporary African urbanization to be seen in its real context. What they amount to is that, most such cities being but a secondary phenomenon, it is not from the town but from the system encompassing it that vitality, force and impetus come. What the town provides is a *milieu* in which, consonant with capitalism's needs, new forms of life and labour may crystallize and take shape (cf. Balandier, 1956). This, in turn, makes it, in Southall's phrase, the 'pace-maker' for the wider society. 'It is there that change proceeds furthest and fastest and economic class considerations most successfully supersede those of tribal origin.' This correctly implies that the alterations taking place are radical in character,[12] but not generated by the town itself. In other words, instead of the town, *per se*, being an innovator, it is the place where change is mainly initiated and the medium through which it passes to the rural countryside.

This diffusion is, in turn, therefore to be regarded as a part of the urbanization process, because it means that the farm or village resident may become 'urbanized' in consequence of the culture of the city being conveyed to him. However, whether urban ideational and behavioural patterns become 'intergrated' into the rural way of life depends upon the extent to which the village as a social organization is itself geared to the urban-industrial economy. This is important because, as we have seen, a frequent practice among labour migrants is regularly to send gifts and remittances back to their kinsfolk at home. The migrant himself looks upon these contributions of cash and commodities as a kind of insurance premium safeguarding, among other things, his right to land. But the general effect of this inflow of money is often more far-reaching. It may serve to underpin the rural economy and so to render traditional institutions more viable than they might otherwise become. As already implied, Tonga society is an example of this. On the other hand, in a situation of this kind it does not necessarily follow that the urbanizing influences of the city are likely to be more than cultural. They usually include the use of new equipment, such as clothing, building materials, household utensils, etc., but do not inevitably involve changes of a structural kind. In other words,

H

although an appreciable proportion of the male population spends most of its working life abroad, these men's return does not alter the traditional system if they simply assume the ordinary role of villagers on retiral.

Generalization, however, is difficult in this regard because of differences in the migrants' behaviour. Thus, according to Schapera, as long ago as the 1940s there were men who, on returning from the South African mines to villages in Bechuanaland, ignored the wishes of their parents and acted on their own impulses. They knew that the older people now depended on them for the money with which to pay taxes and meet other wants and that in consequence they had acquired a new importance in family life to which the old conceptions of discipline must yield. In this kind of situation the significant consideration is not so much the acquisition of so-called urban attitudes, but that the village itself is now involved in the same monetary economy as the town. Thus, as already mentioned, since it is now possible to earn money for themselves, young men are less dependent on their elders for bridewealth. They can raise the amount asked for by their own efforts when they wish to marry.

Of course, in these terms social change in the village is brought about in a general way by the mere fact of labour migration removing the able-bodied young men. Actual food production may not be adversely affected if, as among the Tonga, subsistence agriculture is carried on almost entirely by the women. When, however, heavy work such as clearing of the forest has to be done and the male exodus is considerable, there may be wide-reaching repercussions. Either land is left uncultivated, or the farming household is obliged to pay for labour which in traditional circumstances would be available on a 'by-turn' or communal basis. Further, although few of the new ideas and interests brought back to the village by returning migrants may produce radical changes in its social organization, the young men concerned frequently find ways of increasing their own prestige and freedom of action. The connections set up between village and town by the development of trade may also lead to some significant modifications.

An interesting example of these urbanizing influences occurred among the Afikpo Ibo living between the headquarters of Afikpo Division Ogoja Province, southern Nigeria and the Cross River. The organization of these Afikpo villages being largely based on age grades, the leaders and the judiciary in many local matters are the elders who constitute the most senior age sets. In controlling village life these men have immediately below them an executive grade to supervise the organization of community services, such as building bridges, repairing tracks, etc. Lineages and secret societies also play an important part in village religious and social activities, but in 1944 a different kind of group was brought into being by a number of men trading up and down the Cross River. This was a voluntary association collecting a small monthly due and loaning the accumulated money at low interest rates to the members. A few years later membership was extended to non-traders as well, and the loan system was developed to make money available not only for trading but for farming, title-taking and other activities. In addition, this union concerned itself with non-traditional construction, seeking to improve local amenities in the shape of more hygienic use of water supplies, a bicycle path to the neighbouring market, etc. It also attempted to provide secondary education for village boys and even to build up a secondary school itself.

Known locally as 'meetings', groups of this kind were associated with individual villages, but in 1950 a union based on a group of villages was formed. Calling itself the Afikpo Town Welfare Association (ATWA), this organization employed its own officials and established branches over a wide area. In addition to stimulating interest in a number of more ambitious 'modern' projects and arbitrating in local politics, it also concerned itself with moral issues; for example, it tried to discourage the traditional custom of physically mature unmarried girls wearing only strings of beads around the hips in public. A number of other 'modern' associations, including social and recreational groups and Christian ones, also came into being and had somewhat similar interests (Ottenberg, 1955, pp. 1–14).

Ottenberg's accounts of these developments makes it clear that the younger men mainly responsible for them were aware of the power of the elders. Instead, therefore, of antagonizing them, they worked with the senior age grades and so included the older men in activities that interested them, such as the raising of loans. It is equally obvious, however, that, especially in the ATWA, organization and procedures showed a considerable divergence from traditional culture and provided the younger men with much more scope than they had in that culture. Moreover, not only was the growth of these associations initially prompted largely by men who had recently returned from work in various Nigerian cities, but the 'progressive' aims of them and their followers – literate in the main – were urban-oriented (*ibid.*). Thus, although the associations carried on their activities in relation to the rural social structure, the changes they sought to introduce were alien to the countryside and encouraged, in some cases, the persons concerned to leave it. This was most obvious in the case of the associations' efforts to provide scholarships for deserving village boys. A village took pride in those of its sons who did well at school and university and shared vicariously in their prestige when they won fame in the world outside.[13] Yet, for practical purposes, this was something that could only be achieved by more or less permanent residence in a city.

What we have tried to convey in the above illustration is that the difficulty of predicting the general course of African social change is reflected in the differential effects of urbanization. However, the cardinal consideration being the extent to which both countryside and towns are absorbed within the overall encompassing politico-economic system, it may help finally to place the African urbanization in historical perspective. This can be done by comparing it with the Industrial Revolution because, despite some resemblance to it, there are important dissimilarities.

Thus, as we have explained, the nature of the contemporary urban African growth is accounted for mainly by the influx of rural people, many of whom come and go between countryside and town. Their stake in the latter tends to be limited and although there are some very positive attractions, especially for women migrants, seeking 'independence', the economic advantages of remaining permanently are only marginal except when a person has relatively high educational qualifications. The English cities of the nineteenth century, by contrast, drew their population not from small peasant farmers but largely from agricultual labourers who owned no land and were already dependent on wages before they entered the urban-industrial force. Further, even labouring for the owners of factories, mines and mills had its compensations because it was economically more attractive than conditions in many of the rural areas.[14] This, coupled with the fact that there was no family land on which to fall back, conduced to make English urban settlement much more permanent than in the contemporary African case. A further result of these factors in combination, including the extra food created by industrialization, was that the towns grew quickly in size through natural increases in population as well as through immigration. This, in turn, meant that larger and larger proportions of these English cities' inhabitants were, to a greater extent than in contemporary Africa, persons who had been born in such places and brought up in an entirely urban culture.

It is therefore almost a truism that although the rate of urban growth in Africa at the present time is even more rapid than in nineteenth-century England, urbanization itself[15] is proceeding at a much slower pace. This is not simply because only about one African person in every ten lives in a city of 100,000 inhabitants or more, or because the cultural differences between town and country-side are greater than those existing in pre-Industrial Revolution Europe. Rather is industrialization the crux of the matter because when urban growth in England got under way,[16] the social system was already functioning on a market economy of which cottage manufacturers, in addition to other forms of rural production, formed a part. In Africa, by contrast, the use of money was entirely unknown in many regions until some seventy years ago; and, although industrial activity is intense now in some places, the rate of increase is generally slow and the scale not much larger in many of the areas concerned than that of late eighteenth-century England.

It is this relative lag in economic development, more than any other factor, which makes it difficult to compare urbanization in sub-Saharan Africa with analogous processes of social change elsewhere, including the Latin American countries. There being no criteria whereby what has been called the 'quality' of urban life can be objectively graded, the temptation is to assess the urban situation in terms of population growth. However, as we have tried to show, under contemporary conditions, there are factors other than size or number of cities to be seriously considered. What matters, sociologically, is not the demographic event, but that the urban ethos developing is something novel and is compounded of both modern and traditional social values. Very likely, it is in effect something quite unique to the African scene.

Appendix

Population figures for towns in sub-Saharan Africa

A comparison over decades or near-decades of the populations*

Town	Year	Population	Year	Population
ANGOLA				
Luanda	1940	61,028	1950	158,882
BURUNDI				
Usumbura	1955	(43,318)	1965	(71,000)
CAMEROUN				
Douala	1955	118,964	1965	200,000
Yaounde	1955	(38,000)	1965	101,000
CENTRAL AFRICAN REPUBLIC				
Bangui	1955	(79,900)	1964	111,266
CHAD				
Fort Lamy	1955	(28,000)	1964	(99,000)
CONGO				
Brazzaville	1950	(83,390)	1957	(99,002)
DAHOMEY				
Cotonou	1956	57,072	1965	(111,100)
Porto Novo	1957	(31,500)	1965	(74,500)
ETHIOPIA				
Addis Ababa	1957	(500,000)	1967	644,120
Asmara	1952	(120,000)	1964	(131,000)
FRENCH SOMALILAND				
Djibouti	1954	(31,000)	1963	(41,217)

*All numbers refer to population in towns, except where there is an asterisk which indicates 'urban agglomeration' rather than town population.
Population figures *without* parentheses are census numbers, either national or municipal.
Population figures *with* parentheses are estimates, including the results of sample surveys.
Figures for 1952, 1955, 1957, 1960 and 1962-9 are taken from the *United Nations Demographic Yearbook*, and for 1968 from the Economic Commission for Africa's *Demographic Handbook for Africa*. A few additional figures are from Hance (1970, p. 240), and for South Africa from the South African Institute of Race Relations.

Town	Year	Population	Year	Population
GABON				
Libreville	1957	(17,100)	1967	(57,000)
GHANA				
Accra	1960	337,828	1968	(615,800)
Kumasi	1960	180,642	1968	(281,600)
Sekondi-Takoradi	1960	75,450	1968	128,200
GUINEA				
Conakry	1958	78,388*	1967	(197,267)*
IVORY COAST				
Abidjan	1955	127,585	1964	(282,000)
KENYA				
Mombasa	1948	84,746	1958	(145,600)
Nairobi	1948	72,227	1958	(221,700)
LIBERIA				
Monrovia	1956	41,391	1962	80,992
MADAGASCAR				
Tananarive	1958	(206,324)	1968	(322,885)
MALAWI				
Blantyre-Limbe	1956	(55,000)	1966	(110,000)
MALI				
Bamako	1955	(68,197)	1965	(165,000)
MAURITIUS				
Port Louis	1952	69,693	1962	119,950
MOZAMBIQUE				
Lourenço Marques	1950	93,265	1960	78,530
NIGER				
Niamey	1959	30,030	1968	(78,991)
NIGERIA				
Aba	1963	131,003	1969	(151,923)
Abeokuta	1963	187,292	1969	(217,201)
Ado-Ekiti	1963	157,519	1969	(182,673)
Benin	1963	100,694	1969	(116,744)
Ede	1963	134,550	1969	(156,036)
Enugu	1953	62,764	1963	138,457
Ibadan	1952	459,196	1963	627,379
Ife	1952	110,790	1963	130,050
Ikere-Ekiti	1963	107,216	1969	(124,337)
Ilesha	1963	165,822	1969	(192,302)
Illa	1963	114,688	1969	(133,003)
Ilorin	1963	208,546	1969	(241,849)
Iwo	1952	100,006	1963	158,583
Kaduna	1952	38,794	1963	149,910
Kano	1952	130,173	1963	295,432
Lagos	1959	(350,000)	1969	(841,749)
Maiduguri	1963	139,965	1969	(162,316)
Ogbomosho	1952	139,535	1963	319,881
Onitsha	1963	163,032	1969	(189,067)

Town	Year	Population	Year	Population
Oshogbo	1952	122,728	1963	210,384
Oyo	1963	112,349	1969	(130,290)
Port Harcourt	1963	179,563	1969	(208,237)
Zaria	1963	166,170	1969	(192,706)
RHODESIA				
Bulawayo	1956	94,991	1966	(200,000)
Salisbury	1956	105,796	1966	(172,000)
SENEGAL				
Dakar	1969	(374,700)	1969	(581,000)
SIERRA LEONE				
Freetown	1959	(100,000)	1969	(170,600)
SOMALIA				
Hargesia	1957	(53,000)	1964	(40,255)
Mogadishu	1957	(80,698)	1967	(172,677)
SOUTH AFRICA				
Benoni	1951	94,402	1960	122,502
Bloemfontein	1960	112,606	1970	180,179
Cape Town	1960	508,341	1970	1,096,597
Durban	1960	560,010	1970	843,327
Germiston	1951	115,991	1960	148,102
Johannesburg	1960	1,152,525*	1970	1,432,643
Port Elizabeth	1960	249,211	1970	468,577
Pretoria	1960	303,684	1970	561,703
Springs	1951	119,382	1960	137,253
TANZANIA				
Dar es Salaam	1948	69,227	1967	272,821
Zanzibar	1948	45,284	1967	68,380
TOGO				
Lomé	1957	(39,000)	1968	(90,600)
UGANDA				
Kampala	1959	(123,000)	1969	330,770
UPPER VOLTA				
Bobo-Dioulasso	1961	(53,000)	1966	(68,000)
Ouagadougou	1955	(32,077)	1966	(77,500)
ZAIRE				
Kinsangani	1959	(126,533)	1966	(149,887)
Kinshasa	1957	(380,314)	1967	(901,520)
Luluaburg	1959	(115,049)	1966	(140,897)
Lumumbashi	1955	(169,985)	1966	(233,145)
ZAMBIA				
Kitwe	1963	101,600	1969	179,300
Lusaka	1959	(78,000)*	1969	238,000*
Ndola	1963	(90,000)	1968	(132,000)
ZANZIBAR				
Zanzibar City	1957	(58,000)	1967	(95,000)

Notes

1 The migratory basis of urban growth

1 Also, several Ngoni groups migrated from the south to what are now Zaire and Tanzania between 1800 and 1884; and there were the almost incessant migrations of the Fang in present Cameroon and Gabon, beginning in the later part of the eighteenth century and lasting for about 150 years (Hance, p. 130).

2 In Ghana, for example, Akwapem farmers were migrating from the middle of the nineteenth century to empty lands where they could grow oil palms and subsistence crops, palm products then ranking as the leading cash crop of the area (Colson, 1960).

3 Thus, the construction of new roads, railways and public works, the opening of mines, the development of cash crops, and petty trade all offer opportunities of employment. Not only is there a host of occupations and ways of getting a living alternative to the traditional system, but it is now very much easier to travel to places where money can be earned, using the various new means of transport, including even the aeroplane.

4 Read (*op. cit.*) also makes the important point that in order for migration to occur it is not only necessary for opportunities of acquiring cash to be available, but there must also be a stimulus that creates a demand for a higher standard of living for which the cash is required. In remote areas, therefore, where villages are little affected by the western monetary economy, not many men are away. On the other hand, in areas which are in close contact and where people are aware of higher standards of living, the proportion of men away is likely to be higher if there are no local means of finding cash. This point is reflected in the findings of a survey made of a migration route into Buganda. Of 200 males, 75 per cent said they were coming for a variety of economic reasons – better pay, bridewealth, and money for domestic uses (Richards (ed.), 1953; see also Mitchell, 1961, pp. 259–80).

5 For example, immigration from specific rural areas was apparently encouraged in order to prevent the growth of any single tribal group large enough to dominate the whole city (La Fontaine, 1970, pp. 4–6, 24–6).

6 The modern amenities of the large cosmopolitan cities – electric lighting, large stores and shops, cinemas, bars and dance halls – have a strong appeal for young men and women whose mentality has hitherto been bounded by the bush enclosing their village. Even an upcountry trading station may be impressive, and his first visit to a small town on the railway line connecting Freetown with the interior of Sierra Leone prompted a young migrant to say (Little, 1967b, p. 260):

> I became sort of idiot as we moved along, for I stood to gaze at whatever English-made articles I have ever seen before, for example, cycles, motor cycles and cars. I took a very keen interest in gazing at two-storey buildings, I admired people moving in them, and I often asked my brother whether they would not fall from these.

7 In Freetown, on the other hand, there were plenty of women and everyone looked after himself; many women would take a lover and expect little in the way of presents, while there were others with whom one could have a 'short-time' for 4/– or 5/– (Banton, 1957, p. 57).

8 This does not mean that Nyakusa labourers work hard and save hard and live quiet economical lives until their return home. On the contrary they spend a good deal on clothes, beer and women and in extravagant expenditure in the urban shops; but Gulliver's estimation is that the migrant takes back, on the average, sh.350–400 in cash and perhaps sh.200 in goods (1960, pp. 58–9).

9 See also Max Gluckman's elaboration of these and other relevant aspects of this matter. He remarks in particular: 'all Africans remember the great depression, when the mines closed and thousands of them returned to their tribal homes – as millions of Americans were absorbed back into eking a living in the same crisis' (1960, pp. 66–8). Elkan also points out that in the Belgian Congo, withdrawal from the countryside was in a sense made a condition of certain kinds of employment: the recruiting conditions insisting upon the labourer being accompanied by his wife and family. Once an entire family left their holding in the countryside it ceased to be theirs and ceased to afford them further income or security. The success of stabilization policies in the Congo may therefore be attributable as much to this compulsory severance from the land as to the positive inducements of employers (quoted by Elkan, 1960, p. 303; see also Hailey, 1956, p. 1392).

2 Modern urbanization and its opportunistic undertones

1 Official sources for urban statistics include the *United Nations Demographic Yearbook*, the Economic Commission for Africa's *Demographic Handbook for Africa*, etc. For recent comparisons of urban population see the Appendix and for other relevant information Hanna and Hanna, 1971, pp. 13–19.

2 Ibu Battuta, who was acquainted with the standards of Arab life in the Mediterranean coast, was surprised by the wealth and civilization of East Africa. He describes Kilwa as 'one of the most beautiful and well-

built towns'. A Portuguese visitor at the end of the fifteenth century was equally impressed (cf. Coupland, 1938).

3 There is also a good deal of movement in and about the town itself and it may be increasing. Taking a particular parish of Kampala – Mulago – Gutkind found that in the course of four months about 10 per cent of the local Ganda inhabitants had left it while 17 per cent were new-comers and 8 per cent had returned to it for the second or third time. Also, almost 11 per cent of the residents, most of whom had been in Mulago from nine to thirty months, had moved once since their arrival; 6 per cent had moved twice and 4 per cent more than twice. Over 61 per cent of those who moved within the parish were non-Ganda – when interviews were carried out between November 1957 and March 1958, the intake into the parish amounted to 31 per cent (17 per cent newcomers and 14 per cent returnees), whereas only 12 per cent of those who had been interviewed between November 1953 and March 1954 had left Mulago (Gutkind, 1965, p. 53).

4 See, in particular, Ardener (1961).

5 For some illustrations and implications of these points see Little, 1973a, chs 1, 6.

6 This point will be elaborated in Chapter 7. Among the authors who have commented on it is Balandier (1956, pp. 495–509).

7 Indeed, in the third quarter of the nineteenth century the proportion of Creole children of school age at school in Freetown probably exceeded that of children attending school in British cities.

8 In West Africa, for example, the value of exports rose in the 1950–60 decade by about 70 per cent.

9 As one writer has put it (McQueen, 1969, p. 44): 'It was a period when leaders were able to galvanise eventually successful independence movements behind powerful symbols of independence and unity.'

10 In the British colonies as a whole the number of Africans in senior service positions increased from 171 in 1949 to 1,581 in 1957; but in French West Africa 'Africanization' appears to have been slower. Thus, although the lower ranks on the ladder were occupied almost entirely by Africans in 1958, heads of departments, professional, and technical personnel were no more than a quarter African. Only a handful of Africans held posts of real responsibility where policy decisions were made (Kimble, ed., 1960, pp. 355–7).

11 These figures are based on the period 1948 to 1966, and, overall, female students constitute 11 per cent of the total. Of the women, 58·5 per cent have professional or semi-professional fathers compared to 31·5 per cent in the case of the men. Also, nearly one-third of the men are the sons of farmers, compared to about one in every ten fathers in the case of the women, while six times as many mothers of women students are semi-professional or professional as are mothers of men (Van den Berghe, 1969).

12 As discerned by more than one satirist of the 'new' men's style of life (Achebe, 1966, pp. 41–2):

The first thing critics tell you about our ministers' official

residences is that each has seven bedrooms and seven bathrooms, one for every day of the week. All I can say is that on that first night there was no room in my mind for criticism. I was simply hypnotized by the luxury of the great suite assigned to me. . . .
I had to confess that if I were at that moment made a minister I would be most anxious to remain one for ever.

13 I am indebted to a suggestion made by Dr Malcolm J. Ruel for this expression.

3   Attitudes to work and wage-employment

1 Occupational mobility may occur on the job as well as by changing employers. Thus, Peil found in Ghana that about a fifth of the workers had done more than one type of work for the same employer. Some had held three or four different posts. About a third of them involved work at the same level: a labourer became a watchman or a semi-skilled worker changed from machine to handwork or vice versa. A quarter of the changes involved moving from manual to clerical work and 17 per cent from unskilled to semi-skilled work. Many school leavers who start as low level clerical workers, office boys, levy-collectors for the local council, later go into manual work because it pays more and is no more boring: many rural craftsmen combine farming with self-employment. They farm most of the year and practise their trade in the off-season and in occasional orders. Craftsmen who are not very successful may abandon their trade, at least temporarily, for farming (Peil, 1972).

2 Gutkind (1968) puts the figure as high as between 10 and 20 per cent. However, there is the question of whether the term 'unemployed' means in Africa what it does in western economies, because there are situations in the former context when workers voluntarily or involuntarily engage in work that takes up only a part of their work potential. In other words, although a man's work sheet will show, perhaps, only three or four days worked in the month, he may be 'gainfully' employed the remainder of the time in, say, petty trade (see Birmingham, Neustadt and Omaboe, 1967, pp. 148–9, and Leslie, 1963, pp. 124–5).

3 That the latter fear is not always imaginary but has some basis in fact is indicated in Chapter 1.

4 See, for instance, as an example of Francophone Africa, Hauser's study (1965). His report is based on an inquiry among 2,600 workers in Dakar.

4   Social class and ethnicity

1 This point is also considered in Chapter 7.

2 Peil also found that in Ghana the reason given for rating occupations high or low was centred on the income which the work provided and, to a much lesser extent, the amount of service to the family or community which it involved (1972). Foster (1965, p. 272), too, has confirmed the importance of income in prestige by having students rate a series of occupations by prestige and then rate them again on the amount of

money they think is earned by men doing this work. Non-Ghanaians were more likely to mention money than were Ghanaians and those coming from rural areas mention it more often than those who grew up in Accra. In both positive and negative prestige, the length of time spent in town was inversely related to the proportion mentioning money. It may well be that urban experience fosters awareness of the various aspects of prestige or that money is so important to those who have least of it that other aspects of prestige are ignored.

3 A major difficulty confronting the would-be analyst of 'social class' is that among African informants there is a notable tendency to upgrade not merely one's own occupation, but the general category of occupations in which one finds oneself and holders of authority with whom one customarily deals. According to Gamble, this explains why in many surveys carried out among students the teaching profession gets ranked so highly. In the Mitchell and Epstein (1959) study, for instance, African education officer, secondary school teacher, and headmaster appear in the first five places. Gamble also points out that in a questionnaire administered to Sierra Leone university students, university lecturer was rated as of highest prestige ranking by 25 per cent in a list which included puisne judge, lawyer, member of the House of Representatives, medical practitioner, and independent businessman (Gamble, 1966, pp. 98–108).

In this connection, too, a study of the city of Enugu in Eastern Nigeria provides a slightly ironic slant on the whole situation. The respondents in this case were asked to classify the categories of people they would call deviants; about 80 per cent of them listed politicians and top civil servants as well as prostitutes, robbers and delinquents (Okediji and Opeyemi, 1967, p. 83).

4 Plotnicov also makes the point that, in part, the élite's emulation of European behaviour patterns can be viewed as acts directed at Europeans. Demonstrating that they can meet the cultural standards of Europeans is not only intended to dispel the image of African inferiority, 'it expresses the ambivalence of the élite in wishing on the one hand to be accepted as equals among Europeans and, on the other, in attempting to outdo Europeans at their own skills' (1970, pp. 295–6). This suggestion has important implications for the problems of race relations considered specifically in Chapter 5.

5 The Fulbe (sing. Pullo) are called Fulani in Nigeria, Ghana, and nearby countries; Fulas in Sierra Leone and Gambia; and Foulahs and Peuls in the former French colonies.

6 As Cohen's study (1969) of the Hausa in Ibadan has shown, there are sometimes advantages in retaining traditional habits and organizations for economic purposes.

7 Thus, at the time of Rouch's survey, out of 1,500 questioned in Accra, 1,300 were from a single district – Tillaberry (Rouch, 1954, p. 56).

8 For an elaboration and discussion of this point see, *inter alios*, Banton, 1957, pp. 95–120; Porter, 1963, *passim*; Wallerstein, 1960, pp. 129–39; and Little, 1972.

9 The classic exposition of this important sociological principle is to be found, of course, in Evans-Pritchard's *The Nuer*, 1940.

10 For example, if a person possesses political influence, his weekend may be spent on the verandah of his house, receiving callers in need of assistance and advice, in the same manner as if he were a 'big man' holding court in a rural compound.

11 Simplification lies in the fact that, although relevant in the earlier days of western contact, this dichotomy has less relevance today because, as explained, the present situation is sociologically now more complex.

5 Urbanization and race relations

1 Furnivall's (1939) classical definition of a plural society is 'a society comprising two or more social orders which live side by side, yet without mingling, in one political unit' (p. 446).

Among the several writers who have employed this concept for analytical purposes are Paden, 1970, pp. 242–70; and Kuper, 1967. For a general consideration of the factors involved see Hanna and Hanna, 1971, pp. 167–201; also Parkin, 1969, *passim*.

2 Similar attitudes have been noted in Freetown where, until fairly recently, the term usually applied to a tribal migrant was 'aborigine'. About the northern migrants' reaction in Ghana, Rouch adds the following (p. 60):

The Zabrama, confident in his ancient civilization, regards the Coast man, whether in a dickey or a Jaguar, as a 'Gurunsi', a descendant of the slaves whom Babatu used to exchange for a kola-nut in the market. . . . This proud attitude of the least 'kaya-kaya' in rags toward the lawyer or doctor who brushes him in his car is one of the most extraordinary facets of behaviour it is possible to see in the Gold Coast.

3 For criticism of its sociological validity, see Morris, 1957, pp. 124–5.

4 Thus, on ceremonial occasions the Governor wore his plumed helmet and administrative and other senior civil servants their official uniforms according to rank. On duty, too, there were small but subtle differences in dress. Thus, in his office the Colonial Secretary, for instance, discarded his jacket but wore trousers and a necktie, while the Assistant Secretaries worked in their shirt sleeves and wore shorts instead of long trousers. The Governor, on the other hand, was never seen in public except in a jacket as well as long trousers. Upcountry, the District Commissioner, strolling from his office in the late afternoon, was followed by a policeman bearing the D.C's official topee with its band of ribbon in the colour of the colony. Social custom also had a binding effect, the practice being for guests invited for dinner to arrive at sundown and be regaled with drinks until about 10.30 p.m. Then the host would roar, 'Boy – bring "chop" ', this being the signal for the male guests to move en masse to the bottom of the garden. When they had urinated, dinner was served and the party ended almost as soon as the meal had been eaten.

5 It was also etiquette for visitors to be dressed formally when they called on these officials, garb being according to rank. For instance, if keeping an appointment with an Assistant Secretary there would be nothing wrong in wearing long trousers instead of shorts, but to appear without a necktie would be out of place. Naturally, no one would dream of wearing shorts for a call on the Governor; and Europeans working in the Secretariat left the building an hour or so later than their African subordinates.

6 The head of the forestry department might be a frequent guest at the table of a high-ranking administrative officer, but a member of the railway department seldom dined with an administrative officer of his own status (Bascom, 1949, pp. 353–4) and the niceties of this distinction were of course more significant when there was a question of, say, temporarily sharing quarters. The present writer noticed this, on his first visit to a British West African colony, in the following circumstances. Having become friendly on shipboard with the head of one of the lower ranking departments, he accepted the latter's invitation to stay for a while as a guest in his bungalow. The impropriety of this action was tactfully made plain in a 'fatherly' way by the Acting Colonial Secretary. He pointed out that my presence in the official's house might cause him some financial embarrassment because his salary was smaller than that of administrative officers.

7 In fact, their club subscriptions might be deducted as a matter of course from their salary unless they actually indicated that they did not wish to be members (Proudfoot and Wilson, 1961, pp. 328–34).

8 Though antique in style, the latters' palaces and compounds were very much larger than the ordinary commoner could afford, and the possession of numerous wives and children was actually more meaningful in terms of prestige than the Europeans' amenities.

9 Discussing the relationship of white and black in Ghana, Jahoda points out (1961, p. 111) that:

the ordinary member of a village community will not only accept the distant authority of the whites but will come to regard their position as an essential part of the order of the universe, on which his own life and security rest.

10 There were, of course, incidents as well which brought Africans spontaneously together. In 1947, for instance, a Colonial Office employee of African origin was denied accommodation at the Bristol Hotel, Lagos, because of his colour. Since this prompted the formation of a United Front committee consisting of every influential leader, the immediate effect was that 'all the nationalists now forgot their quarrel in the immediate endeavour to fight this insult to the negro race'. A violent protest included a meeting which condemned in unequivocal terms such designations as 'European hospital', 'European reservation' and 'European club' (Olusanya, 1973, pp. 104–6).

11 In addition to 'Pan-Africanism', concepts such as the 'African Personality' were employed in the Anglophone countries and 'Négritude' in the Francophone ones. In fact, although the purpose of slogans

of this kind was to signify and symbolize African solidarity, they had little appeal outside intellectual circles. One of O'Brien's respondents (see pp. 59–60 below) remarked anent the idea of Négritude being a dialogue between black and white cultures, 'it was President Senghor who created the dialogue, and only he who participated in it' (p. 250). Apologists of these concepts have argued that instead of being simply racism in reverse, they have as their goal the destruction of racism. Thus, according to Jean-Paul Sartre, for example, 'Négritude' is 'anti-racism' (cf. Drake, 1961, pp. 38–51).

12 Zikists were, of course, members of the movement founded by Dr Namdi Azikiwe, probably the most influential leader of West African nationalism in general. The advantage of laying complaints of all kinds at the Europeans' door was that, nationalism apart, it was a useful method of attracting followers to a would-be leader's own standard. It is also significant in this regard that the Zikist movement's campaign was directed not only against British rule but against fellow Nigerians whom its members considered not nationalistic enough (Olusanya, pp. 115–16).

In Ghana, too, the interests of populist nationalism widened the attack to include Africans who, like the chiefs and the élite, were accused of buttressing colonial rule (cf. Coleman and Rosberg, 1964, pp. 208–70).

13 Typical statements were: 'Europeans think Africans are subhuman because of their colour'; 'Generally, they regard us as backward: a few of them regard us as animals'; 'They think we are black monkeys'; 'They treat us like children'; 'They think we are primitive, disregard us, and don't give us promotion'; 'They think we are created to serve them'; 'Whites pity Africans as being less fortunate'; etc.

A further common theme was that Europeans were very lazy and made Africans do the work (Jahoda, 1961, pp. 46–64).

14 The similarity of these attitudes to those of southern whites in the Deep South of the United States will be obvious. In terms of that situation, the 'uppity' Negro is the counterpart of the 'urban' African and the Negro 'who knows his place' that of the 'rural' African.

15 On a ship bound for West Africa a European woman resident in Gambia was overheard explaining to a newcomer that the population of Bathurst was extremely small: 'it amounted to less than 100 people'.

16 Hence the apt title of Mumford's book – *Africans learn to be French*. In effect, the French policy was 'assimilationist', i.e. Africans were to be 'civilized' and then integrated with Europeans as equals within a Euro-African union. In practice, however, assimilation was only applied in the old *communes* of Senegal, and it was later formally abandoned in favour of the former *de facto* policy of 'association'. In the latter an educated African middle class assigned to subaltern positions was created to bridge the gap between the European rulers and the African masses (see Hanna, 1963, p. 16 and pp. 25–6 below).

17 Of Europeans 31 per cent were in administration; 20 per cent in the police; 13 per cent in commerce; the African percentages were respec-

tively 7, 4 and 8. Metal work accounted for 12 per cent of Europeans and 10 per cent of Africans, and 2 per cent of Europeans and 12 per cent of Africans were in unskilled work (Hanna and Hanna, 1971, pp. 113–14).

In this connection, too, it should be noted that it is not only in industrially developed South Africa, with its large European population, that economic relations conform to the general racial hierarchy. Jinja, mentioned above, is a 'boom' town of Uganda in which, as will be explained later, Europeans, Asians and Africans each had their own stereotypes of the other groups.

18 Such a phenomenon did not occur in British Crown Colonies where there was for many years a tacit prohibition on the immigration of Europeans to do work incompatible with the political and social rank of their group (Banton, 1967, p. 243). In fact, any DSB ('distressed British seaman') reaching up on the shores of, say, Sierra Leone, was kept out of public sight as far as possible until there were means of shipping him home.

19 These developments were not limited to Dakar. In many other towns of AOF *petits-blancs* filled the many posts of lower supervisory rank that qualified Africans might have taken over had there not been Europeans present in such numbers. By 1956 some few African university graduates had moved into the higher posts of the civil service, but there were still 5,500 Europeans in the middle ranks, in jobs requiring no more than secondary school training. What was true of the bureaucracy in government was even truer in private industry.

20 In fact, social and economic opportunities for Africans did not keep pace with political advance. Thus, between 1946 and 1958, Africans in AOF secured political power within their territories, but the apparatus of government and the administration of private economic activity remained in the hands of Europeans. There were two kinds of African political leaders – ministers, deputies and their aides – and the rest 'who were still to an extraordinary degree the hewers of wood and the drawers of water. In the middle was a great void, filled by the Frenchmen in Africa' (Berg, 1960).

21 An opposite impression is conveyed by some African novelists. For example, in Ousmane's *God's Bits of Wood* (1960), Frenchmen of the managerial class are, in the eyes of Senegalese illiterate and semi-literate workers, over-bearing, loutish, and wholly without sympathy for Africans. There is also Oyono's *Houseboy* (1960), written from the point of view of an African domestic servant, which provides a similar stereotype. However, the latter book's *locale* is the former French Cameroons and not Senegal, while Ousmane wrote about Senegalese relationships within the context of a very bitter industrial dispute. For this reason Dr O'Brien feels that the attitudes described are barely germane except to that particular event (personal communication from Dr O'Brien).

22 This was the opinion, for example, of ten out of twenty-five middle class people living on a housing estate whom O'Brien interrogated

specifically about this matter. Some of these respondents remarked, significantly, that Frenchmen were no longer able openly to display their racism (p. 263), and it is possible that a larger sample – particularly of students and articulate civil servants – might have revealed more potential hostility to the French (personal communication from Dr O'Brien).

23 Personal communication from Dr O'Brien.

24 It naturally follows that the contrast between this situation and the one thirty or forty years earlier is considerable. Thus, in the *Diary of a Colonial Officer's Wife* the author describes numerous meetings with her husband's colleagues, but does not record a single social contact with Africans (Boyd, 1970). This was in the then Gold Coast during the 1914–18 war when, of course, there were far fewer educated Africans about than today.

25 This club ran an annual and usually successful dance to which invitations were customarily sent to the 'Commanding Officer and his Officers'. However, after an African of commissioned rank and his wife had also arrived to join in the fun, this practice of asking the officers as a group was given up. In fact, although several members of the club were on friendly and intimate terms with Africans, efforts to admit the latter even as guests were foiled (Proudfoot and Wilson, 1961).

26 In fact, once the colonial government had accepted 'Africanization', colour bars in government-administered establishments only operated until they were challenged. In one such organization, when two African friends of the present writer were refused service, the Colonial Secretary was informed and the restaurant concerned was given prompt orders to serve Africans as well as European customers. Numbers of European-owned mining companies providing their managerial and technical staff with social amenities took a similar step. Management simply laid it down that these were open to all Africans and Europeans above a particular grade and this settled the matter. The ruling applied to women employees as well as men, and so if European nurses, for example, were eligible, so were their African colleagues.

27 'Genuine' European clubs are, however, not entirely defunct in West Africa. A company club in Ghana, for example, serves the needs of some forty expatriates working for a mining enterprise and has 'an opportunity for the release of vast amounts of nervous energy as its prime purpose' (Robertson, 1971, pp. 207–18).

28 By this is meant that Africans and Europeans are consciously alive to the existence of racial (biological) differences between each other as groups, and that this recognition of racial differences plays some part, at least, as a factor in social relationships between individual Africans and Europeans (cf. Little, 1953, pp. 6–7).

29 In one such case an Englishman, well known in the United Kingdom for his liberal attitude towards Africans, chanced to include in a *New Statesman* article a few phrases regarded as derogatory by the government of the African country where, as it happened, he was living at the time and occupying a senior academic position.

120

30 Consonant with traditional stereotypes of Europeans as a socially superior class, value is attached to neatness and tidiness in dress, and some white people, such as members of the American Peace Corps, have been unfavourably received on account of their 'scruffy' appearance. To dress casually in jeans, etc., may be *de rigueur* from the point of view of the young voluntary workers concerned, but in African eyes it connotes low social status in somewhat similar terms to the American Negro expression 'poor white trash'.

31 There were therefore some important differences between people of various educational levels. People with an education beyond the elementary level had a great deal in common with Europeans and shared many of their basic values, which made for harmony and understanding. Illiterates lived in another world which overlapped very little with that of whites. Also, the fact that illiterate women gave the largest proportion of 'like' responses is to be understood in the fact that, unlike the men, only one of the women had at some time or another been employed by Europeans, or under their supervision (Jahoda, 1961, pp. 56–60).

32 In contrast, according to Mumford (1936), Africans aspiring to be 'French' were given the impression that French culture – the French way of life – had a special quality which made it worth possessing for its own sake.

33 As an East African writer has put it, 'the development of African nationalism is a progressive metamorphosis of what would be an adequate expression of racial equality' (Mazrui, 1963, p. 96).

34 See above and O'Brien, *passim*. The point she makes and has stressed in a personal communication is that those Senegalese who have been brought up in the French idiom tended to develop a kind of psychological as well as cultural dependence upon French society.

35 The many authors who have dealt with this matter in terms somewhat similar to the above set of factors include, in particular, Barnes, 1955; Gray, 1960; Hatch, 1962; Simons and Simons, 1969; and Van der Horst, 1965.

36 For example, in the East African countries of Kenya, Uganda, Zanzibar and Tanganyika (now Tanzania), there were in the 1950s only some 198,000 Indians compared with 18 million Africans. Arabs numbered some 79,000 and Europeans some 50,000 (Morris, 1956, p. 194). By the early 1960s these countries had between them a total population of some 25 millions, of whom some 351,000 were Asians, mostly Indians (estimated from tables in Banton, 1967, pp. 214–21).

37 Most of the original inhabitants of Nairobi, for example, were Indians, and Indians constituted nearly a third of Nairobi's population until as late as 1961. By 1969, however, the Indian percentage had dropped to some 13 per cent and the African risen to some 83.

38 This also applies in large measure to Indians in the nearby countries of Zambia, Rhodesia and Malawi (see Dotson and Dotson, 1968).

39 This has remained the case, especially in the largest towns and despite the ever-increasing movements of Africans into them. As recently as

1969, not only were Asians the most urbanized group in Kenya, but some 76 per cent of its Asian population lived in Nairobi and Mombasa (Tiwari, 1972).

40 Sofer points out that the virtual absence of skilled African artisans was due largely to prestige considerations. In other words, those Africans best fitted by virtue of their formal training to profit from technical training preferred clerical employment, even at lower rates of pay (1956, p. 605).

41 Winder's tentative estimation (1961–2) is that the Lebanese and Syrian communities in West Africa (including both the Anglophone and Francophone countries) totalled somewhere in the neighbourhood of 11,000 to 12,000, if only the foreign born were counted. It would amount to between 30,000 and 40,000 if children and grandchildren are included. The present population of Nigeria alone is probably more than 60 million, and the numerical insignificance of the Lebanese may be further seen in a more recent estimate that in Sierra Leone there are only slightly more than 3,000 in a total population of some 2,200,000, i.e. less than 0·002 per cent (cf. Stanley, 1970, p. 159).

It should also be noted that although referred to officially by their proper nationality, the Lebanese are spoken of colloquially as 'Syrians'. Syrians are, in fact, even fewer in number, but this writer cannot recall the term 'Lebanese' itself being used in conversation at any time during his own stay in the West Coast (see also Winder, 1961–2, f.n., p. 298).

42 Hence the term 'coral men' by which they were often called (Hanna, 1958).

43 This is particularly evident in Sierra Leone where, in the earlier days of the Protectorate, it was difficult for travellers and goods to move upcountry except by train.

44 For an illustration of this point in the context of Sierra Leone, see Stanley's figure (1970, p. 164). Stanley also provides some contemporary case studies of these operations as carried on upcountry by Lebanese families, including diamond dealers (pp. 167–71).

45 See Khuri, 1962, p. 389.

46 Winder provides statistics which show that in this process the Lebanese had out-distanced their European competitors even by 1935 (p. 309).

47 According to reports, the largest trucking firm was paid £1,000,000 when it sold out to a government agency.

48 See Bauer, 1954, *passim*, in this connection.

49 For a clear exposition of this kind of stereotype see Graham Greene's novel, *The Heart of the Matter* (1948).

50 See also Winder (p. 297) on this point.

51 Vol. 2, no. 37 (14 May 1959), p. 2 (quoted by Winder, p. 322).

52 For an example of one such apparent indiscretion, involving charges made by the powerful Action Group political party in Nigeria, see Winder, pp. 327–9.

53 On Lebanese association football teams and other sport activities, see Muruwah, 1938, pp. 221, 225, 228 (cited by Winder, p. 323).

The present writer recalls refereeing a match in an upcountry town in

Sierra Leone between teams, one of whom had a young Lebanese trader as both manager and player.

54 According to Winder, all the Lebanese in Northern Nigeria speak Hausa, and there are some in the western part of the country who can give formal speeches in Yoruba. A Lebanese in Dakar even composes poetry in Wolof (p. 322).

55 An earlier example was the violence that erupted in Freetown in 1919 when mobs attacked Lebanese store-homes. So grave was the threat to Lebanese lives that the government had to house and feed the community for a month and a half thereafter, although it had apparently taken no precautions to ward off the blow, despite previous warning signs (Winder, 1961–2, p. 300).

56 Especially where both parents of an individual born in the country were Lebanese. Where one parent was Lebanese and one African, their citizenship had never seriously been in question. Nevertheless, when the son of a Lebanese father and an African mother tried to enter government service, he found the path blocked. It required a decision by the Judicial Committee of the Privy Council in London to open the way. This was in 1969, before Sierra Leone declared itself a Republic.

6 Urban social organization

1 For a detailed description of the history and functioning of Freetown's tribal administration, see Banton, 1957, chapter 2.

2 See also Chapter 7 in this connection.

3 In referring to Nyasaland we write in the historical present because Mitchell's study was published before independence when Nyasaland became Malawi.

4 The name 'Chanda' is a pseudonym, and the other characters have been given English names for convenience.

5 A vernacular expression used of one considered to have severed his ties with his village completely.

6 The conclusion, therefore, that Ganda society in Mulago rests on kin-based networks suggests an adaptation of the rural family to urban conditions because the Ganda social unit in Mulago appears to be as small as households in other 'modern' African towns. Thus, although there are other combinations, typically consists of a man and wife and children or a man and his older children. This is comparable with the average number of persons reported for households in Kumasi (3·84), Lagos (3·9), Freetown (3·9) and a squatter settlement in Lusaka (almost 6) (Little and Price, 1974).

7 In Lagos, for example, 70 per cent of heads of households gave some regular help to at least one member of their natal family, 55 per cent of them gave an average of over £1 (out of a monthly average earning of £20); 25 per cent spent regularly £4 on relatives, and 12 per cent £6. These sums did not include family ceremonies (Marris, 1961, pp. 36–8).

8 Much of the extensive literature of this subject, including extra-

marital relationships, is drawn on and references to it cited in Little, 1973a.

9 For a typology of urban households see Little and Price, 1974.

10 Compulsory national insurance, in its elementary form, is now being introduced in Kenya, Tanzania and Uganda. The aim is to provide benefit at the age of 60 or 65 or whenever an employee is incapacitated (Jellicoe, 1968, p. 19).

11 A more militant form of messianic movement was founded in the Lower Congo by Simon Kimbangou, a Christian catechist. He claimed to have been sent by God with a special revelation for the African race, and the idea that he would return as the 'saviour and king of black people' and liberate them from the colonial yoke was kept alive and gave rise to quite an elaborate organization of syncretistic churches (Balandier, 1953; Comhaire, 1955).

12 Also prominent is the revivalistic character of their worship which includes speaking with tongues, spirit possession and the interpretation of dreams and visions. In the services there is complete congregational participation in the form of hand-clapping, dancing and sometimes drumming, spontaneous singing and pious ejaculation. Other common elements include a special interest in faith-healing, in the exorcism of malevolent spirits by prayers, fastings, sprinkling with 'holy' water, and anointing with oil.

13 All members wear a small wooden crucifix around the neck and are obliged to fast every Friday, taking only water and chewing kola from dawn to dusk; longer fasts up to seven days are prescribed for the clergy. There is a taboo on sexual intercourse and on indecent conversation during fast periods. Alcohol, tobacco, pork and 'blood' are forbidden, and menstruous women do not join in services of worship although their participation is not forbidden. Members are not allowed to consult either western-trained doctors or African herbalists, and resorting to a medicine man or to magical healing of any kind is punishable by prompt exclusion from the church (Parrinder, 1953, pp. 107–32; Smith, 1963; Baëta, 1962; Sundkler, 1961).

14 As in the case of Ibo contributions clubs. These meet every eighth day, i.e. once every Ibo week, and include some four different types. The first group consists of people who belong to the same local unit. Another type is that in which the organizers belong to a professional or trade group; and a third type of club is organized within an existing association, such as an age-grade. Lastly, there are those contribution clubs which are organized by women. Quite often there is a series of officials, viz. council members for judging real or fictitious disputes during meetings, council messengers to call witnesses, checkers to count the money, dividers to share the wine and food among members, and so forth (cf. Ardener, 1953, pp. 132–3).

15 For a short but detailed example see Imoagene (1967, pp. 51–66).

16 In fact, although the members of a particular union speak of themselves in tribal terms, membership qualifications are relatively liberal. Thus membership of the Luo Union in Kampala 'is open to . . . all adult

Luo men and women ... any other adult person other than Luo who lives within the Luo community and agrees with Luo customs and traditions and with its constitution' (Parkin, 1969, pp. 151–2). For further information about location and other associations in Kampala, see Jellicoe, 1968.

17 Parkin draws attention to this hierarchy of associations (1966b, pp. 90–5), pointing out that all the organizations concerned are formed by members of uncentralized tribes, whose rural structures are that of the localized, polysegmentary lineage type (that is, lineages that have many segments or branches). Migrants from centralized tribes are already familiar with both political and economic specialization and relatively marked socio-economic status systems. They have little need to reorganize themselves for urban living and do not, therefore, establish tribal associations. Problems of mutual aid continue to be referred to informal networks of kin and others. Migrants from egalitarian societies, on the other hand, are unfamiliar with urban status systems. Parkin suggests, therefore, that among the uncentralized tribes the unintended or latent function of each intratribal hierarchy of associations is to provide a framework of socio-economic differentiation. This serves, in ways that are indicated below, as an institution of adaptation.

Tribal unions among uncentralized peoples in Nigeria have also undergone several phases of integration. These involved, respectively, the federation of all branches abroad of the same union, the federation of the federated branches abroad with the same branch, and the formation of an all-tribal federation. This process resulted in a pyramidal structure for the all-tribal federation, and it began with the primary associations (the extended family among the Ibo) and passed upward through the various levels of the social structure (clan), or of the territorial organization (division of province) of the tribe concerned (Little, 1965, pp. 34f.).

18 Also, the aim being to strengthen group solidarity by encouraging members' attachment to their native town or lineage, every effort is made to foster and keep alive an interest in the moral beliefs, language, song and history of the tribe. Some associations go so far as to record these things in writing for the benefit of the younger generation, who have never known the older customs (Little, 1965).

19 For consideration of this point see Little, 1965.

20 Quite often, local chiefs and other notables help with funds, and the home association embarks on its own regular programme of activities. There are football matches and dances to attract people from the larger towns; and communal work, such as building bridges or repairing roads, is also undertaken (Little, 1965, pp. 29–30).

21 Apparently, a ruling of this kind was so effective that, in Nigeria, Ibo people entirely deserted the courts, except when drawn there by members of different tribes or in the rare event of disloyalty on the part of a member of their own union. The members of another Nigerian tribal union resolved not to marry any girl of their town so long as the

prevailing amount of money asked for bridewealth was not reduced (Offodile, 1947).

22 The more established associations tend, in fact, to be very careful about whom they admit, and they inquire into an applicant's background and credentials. This is the practice of voluntary associations in general. For example, one of the recreational groups in Sierra Leone, known as dancing *compins* (*compin* is the Krio word for 'company'), claims that it accepts fewer than half the people who want to become members. The better known *compins* also co-operate with one another, transferring members on request, while if an applicant has formerly belonged to another *compin*, he will not obtain admission into the new one until it has communicated with the one he has left (Offodile, 1947, pp. 939, 941; Banton, 1957, p. 174).

7 Conclusions

1 One such example, despite extensive new constructions, is Lagos where office buildings and banks and occasionally well-to-do homes line the frontages of the 'down-town' streets 'like concrete dams blocking the indigenous tide of life welling behind them' (Little, 1965, pp. 35–6).

2 In this Cameroons situation, as in the modern town itself, a woman, nowadays, is in a position to gather money from prostitution sufficient to repay her bridewealth herself. The chief ground for divorce given by women is lack of proper maintenance by the husband; but this has become little more than a cliché. Husbands may divorce their wives for adultery or on other grounds, but in practice it is the women who precipitate divorce by running away. In fact, among Bakweri women of the indigenous tribe, frequent divorces, interspersed with periods of concubinage and prostitution, have become as much a habit of life as labour migration has become to the men of other tribes. One in six of the women in extant unions in Ardener's sample were in illegitimate unions, about equally divided between concubines and true prostitutes. Twenty-six per cent of those in this group of women who were between 30 and 34 years of age were in illegitimate unions and 11 per cent in prostitution (Ardener, 1961).

3 See, *inter alios*, Mitchell and Shaul, 1965, pp. 625–33.

4 This pattern of town-village relationship has several parallels in other parts of West Africa. In the case of the Nupe of Nigeria, for example, the concentration of a large population in a single town leads to the formation of 'daughter settlements' by small groups. These 'colonies' are known as *tunga* and normally they reflect the expansion rather than the breaking up of the 'mother town'. The phenomenon takes several forms: small groups move in inhabited bush, to occupy virgin land and to form new settlements; immigrants from another part of the country choose to settle on land which belongs to a certain village and under its political protection; or the big landlords settle

their shares and dependants on the land around the capital, in small hamlets (Nadel, 1942, p. 36).

5 Hance (1970) makes the somewhat similar point that the pre-eminence of trading-commercial cities and inland ports reflects the degree to which the modern economies of Africa are oriented to international trade.

6 What is surprising in this regard is that in tropical Africa there are relatively few mining towns with populations exceeding 20,000, and all of those with 100,000 inhabitants are associated with the Katanga-Copper Belt complex (Hance, 1970).

7 For a lucid exposition of neo-colonialism from the point of view of a well-known African nationalist, see Nkrumah, 1965.

8 For example, according to a recent study, although there has been some diminution, the trade of the West African countries is still mainly with Paris and London rather than with other countries in Africa. The same applies to the volume of telegraphic and telephonic communications with the exception of connections between Dakar and Bathurst and Conakry and Dakar (cf. Adams, 1972).

9 The control of the former Belgian Congo by great financial interests is one of the best-known examples of this, and such companies have often been accused not only of supporting reactionary governments in the developing countries, but of seeking to protect their investments by political means in the developed countries as well. In fact (at a seminar organized by Kirkcaldy Town Council, Scotland, to mark the 250th anniversary of the birth of Adam Smith; cf. *Scotsman*, 7 June 1973) J. K. Galbraith has said of this kind of international corporation, '[it] is a polar force in our age. It controls prices and costs, organizes supplies, persuades consumers, guides the Pentagon, seeks to buy presidents, and is otherwise a dominant influence in the state.'

10 In fact, only a few towns in tropical Africa are mainly concerned with manufacturing and this is in line with the neo-colonial situation. Thus, Guinea's politico-economic strategy has been operated well enough to allow its government and ruling party to sustain both power and a fairly wide base of support for well over a decade, despite the very severe shock of total French withdrawal. 'Neo-capitalism and (in relation to Paris) neo-provincialism have been implemented with considerable skill and quite dramatic short-term pay-off in the Ivory Coast. An apparently comparable set of aims in Liberia has produced far poorer results' (Green, 1970, p. 275).

11 I say 'individually' because although Nigeria, for example, is now ranked as a 'middle power', it is only in terms of their constituting a collective force, such as the OAU, that African countries can usually be regarded as politically on a par with more than a few of the developed countries.

12 Using the concept of 'radical' or 'structural' change precisely as formulated by Raymond Firth (1959, pp. 346ff.).

13 Achebe provides a clear illustration of this point in chapter 1 of his novel *A Man of the People* (1966) (cited in note 12 of Chapter 2).

14 In fact, even labourers' wages in the towns were higher than those in the countryside. In 1824, when northern farm wages averaged 11*s*. 7*d*. a week, those for labourers in Manchester and Bradford were 13*s*. and 16*s*. respectively. Perhaps the cost of living in the towns was higher, and rents certainly were, but the difference in wages was still wide enough to attract a steady flow of immigrants from the countryside (Perkin, 1969, pp. 132–3).

15 Our distinction between urbanization as a social process and urban population growth was made in the Introduction.

16 This was during the first half of the nineteenth century. In 1801 only a third of the population lived in a town of any size. By 1831 half the population lived in towns, and more than a fifth in towns over 100,000 inhabitants (Perkin, 1969, p. 117).

Further reading

AJAEGBU, H. I. (1972) (ed.) *African Urbanization: A Bibliography*, London: International African Institute. Provides probably the most complete list to date of literature dealing with specific towns.

CENTRE OF AFRICAN STUDIES, University of Edinburgh (1963) *Urbanization in African Social Change*, Edinburgh. Provides a short but compact study of African urban social structure in articles by some twenty well-known authors.

GRILLO, R. D. (1973) *African Railway Men: Solidarity and Opposition in an East African Labour Force*, Cambridge University Press. A useful analysis of the 'work' situation.

MINER, HORACE (1953) *The Primitive City of Timbucktoo*, Princeton University Press. One of the few complete studies available of a 'traditional' town, based on actual fieldwork.

MINER, HORACE (1967) (ed.) *The City in Modern Africa*, New York: Praeger. A collection of articles dealing with various aspects of African urbanism from different standpoints.

MITCHELL, J. CLYDE (1966) 'Theoretical Orientations in African Urban Studies', in M. Banton (ed.), *The Social Anthropology of Complex Societies*, London: Tavistock. A useful discussion of methodology in African urban studies, including the important distinction between 'processive' and 'situational' change.

UNESCO (1956) *Social Implications of Industrialization and Urbanization in Africa South of the Sahara*, Paris. Although somewhat dated, this is still useful as a general source book of relevant information and research procedures.

WOOD, E. W. (1968) 'The implications of migrant labour, for urban social systems', *Cahiers d'Etudes Africaines*, 8, 29. A useful discussion of this relevant factor in urbanization.

Bibliography

ACHEBE, CHINUA (1966) *A Man of the People*, London: Heinemann.
ACKAH, C. A. (1969) 'Social stratification in Ghana', *Ghana Journal of Sociology*, 5 (2).
ACQUAH, IONE (1958) *Accra Survey*, University of London Press.
ADAMS, JOHN G. U. (1972) 'External linkages of national economies in West Africa', *African Urban Notes*, VI (3).
AJAYI, J. F. A. and CROWDER, MICHAEL (1971) *History of West Africa*, vol. 1, London: Longman.
ALLDRIDGE, T. J. (1910) *A Transformed Colony*, London: Seeley.
ARDENER, E. W. (1961) 'Social and Demographic Problems of the Southern Cameroons Plantation Area', in A. W. Southall (ed.), *Social Change in Modern Africa*, London: Oxford University Press for International African Institute.
ARDENER, SHIRLEY (1953) 'The Social and Economic Significance of the Contribution Club, among a Section of the Southern Ibo', *Proceedings* (Annual Conference), Ibadan: West African Institute of Social and Economic Research.
ASSOCIATION OF COMMONWEALTH UNIVERSITIES, *Commonwealth Universities Yearbook*, London.
BAËTA, C. G. (1962) *Prophetism in Ghana*, London: CM.
BALANDIER, GEORGES (1953) 'Messianismes et nationalismes en Afrique noire', *Cahiers Internationaux de Sociologie*, 7 (1).
BALANDIER, GEORGES (1955) *Sociologie des Brazzavilles Noires*, Paris: Colin.
BALANDIER, GEORGES (1956) 'Urbanism in West and Central Africa: The Scope and Aims of Research', in International African Institute, *Social Implications of Industrialization and Urbanization in Africa South of the Sahara*, Paris: UNESCO.
BANDOH, A. A. (n.d.) Unpublished manuscript.
BANTON, MICHAEL P. (1954) 'Tribal headmen in Freetown', *Journal of African Administration*, 6, 3.
BANTON, MICHAEL P. (1957) *West African City*, London: Oxford University Press.
BANTON, MICHAEL P. (1967) *Race Relations*, London: Tavistock.

130

BARNES, J. A. (1954) 'Class and committees in a Norwegian island parish', *Human Relations*, 7.

BARNES, J. A. (1955) 'Race Relations in the Development of Southern Africa', in A. W. Lind (ed.), *Race Relations in World Perspective*, Honolulu: University of Hawaii Press.

BASCOM, WILLIAM R. (1949) 'West and Central Africa', in Ralph Linton (ed.), *Most of the World*, London: Oxford University Press.

BASCOM, WILLIAM R. (1955) 'Urbanization among the Yoruba', *American Journal of Sociology*, LX (5).

BASCOM, WILLIAM R. (1959) 'Urbanism as a Traditional African Pattern', in Kenneth Little (ed.), *Urbanism in West Africa, Sociological Review*, 7 (N.S.).

BASCOM, WILLIAM R. (1963) 'The urban African and his world', *Cahiers d'Etudes Africaines*, 4 (14).

BAUER, PETER (1954) *West African Trade*, Cambridge University Press.

BERG, ELLIOT J. (1960) 'The economic basis of political choice in French West Africa', *American Political Review*, LIV.

BETTISON, D. G. (1961) 'Changes in the Composition and Status of Kin Groups in Nyasaland and Northern Rhodesia', in A. W. Southall (ed.), *Social Change in Modern Africa*, London: Oxford University Press for International African Institute.

BIRD, MARY (n.d.) 'Social Change and Kinship and Marriage among the Yoruba of Western Africa', unpublished PhD thesis, Edinburgh University.

BIRMINGHAM, W. I., NEUSTADT, I., and OMABOE, E. N. (1967) *A Study of Contemporary Ghana*, vol. 2, Evanston, Ill.: Northwestern University Press.

BOSERUP, ESTER (1970) *Women's Role in Economic Development*, London: Allen & Unwin.

BOVILL, E. W. (1933) *Caravans of the Old Sahara*, London: Oxford University Press for International African Institute.

BOYD, LAURA (1970) *Diary of a Colonial Officer's Wife*, London: Collins.

BREESE, GERALD (1966) *Urbanization in Newly Developing Countries*, Englewood Cliffs, New Jersey: Prentice-Hall.

BUSIA, K. A. (1950) *Social Survey of Sekondi-Takoradi*, Accra: Government Printer.

BUTCHER, D. A. P. (1964) 'The Role of the Fulbe in the Urban Life and Economy of Lunsar, Sierra Leone', unpublished PhD thesis, Edinburgh University.

CAREY, A. T. (n.d.) unpublished study of Keta, Gold Coast, Department of Social Anthropology, Edinburgh University.

CHARLES, PIERRE (1952) 'Tribal society and labour legislation', *International Labour Review*, LXV (4).

CHRISTENSEN, JAMES BOYD (1962) 'The Adaptive Functions of Fanti Priesthood', in W. R. Bascom and M. J. Herskovits (eds), *Continuity and Change in African Cultures*, University of Chicago Press.

COHEN, ABNER (1969) *Custom and Politics in Urban Africa*, London: Routledge & Kegan Paul.

COLEMAN, JAMES S. and ROSBERG, CARL G. (1964) (eds) *Political Parties and National Integration in Tropical Africa*, Berkeley: University of California Press.

COLSON, ELISABETH (1960) 'Migration in Africa: Trends and Possibilities', in F. Lorimer and M. Karp (eds), *Population in Africa*, Brookline, Mass.: Boston University Press.

COMHAIRE, JEAN (1955) 'Sociétés secrètes et mouvements prophétiques au Congo Belge', *Africa*, XXV (1).

COUPLAND, REGINALD (1938) *East African Invaders*, Oxford: Clarendon Press.

COX, OLIVER CROMWELL (1948) *Caste, Class and Race*, New York: Doubleday.

DAVIS, KINGSLEY (1968) 'The Urbanisation of the Human Population', in Sylvia Fleis Fava (ed.), *Urbanism in World Perspective*, New York: Crowell.

DAWSON, JOHN (1964) 'Race and inter-group relations in Sierra Leone', *Race*, VI, Oct., 2.

DOTSON, FLOYD and LILIAN O. (1968) *The Indian Minority of Zambia, Rhodesia and Malawi*, New Haven, Conn.: Yale University Press.

DOUCHY, A. and FELDHEIM, P. (1956) 'Some Effects of Industrialization in Equatoria Province', in *Social Implications of Industrialization and Urbanization in Africa South of the Sahara*, Paris: UNESCO.

DRAKE, ST CLAIR (1961) 'Pan-Africanism, Négritude and the African personality', *Boston University Graduate Journal*, X.

EKWENSI, CYPRIAN (1961) *Jagua Nana*, 4th ed., London: Hutchinson.

ELKAN, W. (1956) *An African Labour Force, East African Studies*, no. 7, East African Institute of Social Research.

ELKAN, W. (1960) *Migrants and Proletarians*, London: Oxford University Press.

EPSTEIN, A. L. (1961) 'The network and urban social organization', *Rhodes-Livingstone Journal*, 29.

EPSTEIN, A. L. (1967) 'Urbanization and social change in Africa', *Current Anthropology*, 8.

EVANS-PRITCHARD, E. (1940) *The Nuer*, Oxford: Clarendon Press.

FEDERAL DEPARTMENT OF STATISTICS, NIGERIA (1957) *Urban Consumer Surveys.*

FIAWOO, D. K. (1959) 'The Influence of Contemporary Social Changes on the Magico-Religious Concepts and Organization of the Southern Ewe-Speaking People of Ghana', unpublished PhD thesis, Edinburgh University.

FIRTH, RAYMOND (1959) 'Social organization and social change', *Journal of the Royal Anthropological Institute*, 84, 1 and 2.

FORTES, MEYER (1945) 'The impact of the war on British West Africa', *International Affairs*, XXI (2).

FORTES, MEYER (1947) 'Ashanti survey, 1945–46: an experiment in social research', *Geographical Journal*, CX.

FOSTER, P. J. (1965) *Education and Social Change in Ghana*, London: Routledge & Kegan Paul.

FRAENKEL, MESSAN (1964) *Tribe and Class in Monrovia*, London: Oxford University Press for International African Institute.

FURNIVALL, J. S. (1939) *Netherlands Indies*, Cambridge University Press.

GAMBLE, D. P. (1963) 'The Temne family in a modern town (Lunsar) in Sierra Leone', *Africa*, XXXIII (3).

GAMBLE, D. P. (1966) 'Occupational prestige in an urban community (Lunsar) in Sierra Leone', *Sierra Leone Studies* (N.S.), 19.

GLUCKMAN, MAX (1960) 'Tribalism in modern British Central Africa', *Cahiers d'Etudes Africaines*, 1.

GOLDTHORPE, J. E. (1955) 'An African élite', *British Journal of Sociology*, 6 (1).

GOLDTHORPE, J. E. (1956) 'Social class and education in East Africa', *Transactions*, 3rd World Congress of Sociology.

GRAY, RICHARD (1960) *The Two Nations*, London: Oxford University Press.

GREEN, REGINALD (1970) 'Political Independence and the National Economy: An Essay in the Political Economy of Decolonization', in Christopher Allen and R. W. Johnson (eds), *African Perspectives*, Cambridge University Press.

GULLIVER, P. H. (1958) 'Land tenure and social change among the Nyakusa', *East African Studies*, 11, East African Institute of Social Research.

GULLIVER, P. H. (1960) 'Incentives in labour migration', *Human Organization*, 19.

GUTKIND, PETER C. W. (1962) 'African urban family life', *Cahiers d'Etudes Africaines*, 10.

GUTKIND, PETER C. W. (1965) 'African urbanism, mobility and the social network', *International Journal of Comparative Sociology*, VI (1).

GUTKIND, PETER C. W. (1968) 'The Poor in Urban Africa', in G. W. Bloomberg and H. J. Schmandt (eds), *Power, Poverty and Urban Policy*, Beverly Hills: Sage.

HAILEY, LORD (1939) *An African Survey*, London: Oxford University Press.

HAILEY, LORD (1956) *An African Survey* (rev. ed.), London: Oxford University Press.

HANCE, W. A. (1970) *Population, Migration and Urbanization in Africa*, New York: Columbia University Press.

HANNA, MARWAN (1958) The Lebanese in West Africa', *West Africa*, nos 2142–3, 26 April, 3 May, 17 May.

HANNA, WILLIAM J. (1963) 'Introduction: The Politics of Freedom', in William J. Hanna (ed.), *Independent Black Africa*, Chicago: Rand McNally.

HANNA, WILLIAM J. and JUDITH L. (1971) *Urban Dynamics in Black Africa*, Chicago: Aldine.

HATCH, JOHN (1962) *Africa Today and Tomorrow*, London: Dobson.

HAUSER, A. (1965) *Rapport d'enquête sur les travailleurs des industries manufacturières de la région de Dakar*, Dakar, Senegal: Institut Français d'Afrique Noire.

HEISLER, HELMUTH (1971) 'The African work force in Zambia', *Civilizations*, XXI (4).

HOLAS, B. (1954) 'Bref aperçu sur les principaux cultes syncrétiques de la basse Côte d'Ivoire', *Africa*, XXIV (1).

HUTCHINSON, JOSEPH (1968) 'Reflections on African development', Presidential address to the African Studies Association of the United Kingdom.

IMOAGENE, STEPHEN O. (1967) 'Mechanisms of immigrant adjustment in a West African community (Sapele town)', *Nigerian Journal of Economic and Social Studies*, 9 (1).

IZZETT, ALISON (1961) 'Family Life among the Yoruba in Lagos, Nigeria', in A. W. Southall (ed.), *Social Change in Modern Africa*, London: Oxford University Press for International African Institute.

JAHODA, GUSTAV (1955) 'The social background of a West African student population', *British Journal of Sociology*, (5) 4 and (6) 1.

JAHODA, GUSTAV (1961) *White Men: A Study of Attitudes of Africans to Europeans in Ghana before Independence*, London: Oxford University Press.

JELLICOE, MARGUERITE (1968) 'Indigenous savings associations in Eastern Africa', Economic Commission for Africa, E/CN. 14 HOU 21.

KHURI, FUAD (1962) 'Kinship, emigration and trade partnership among the Lebanese of West Africa', *Africa*, XXXV (3).

KIMBLE, GEORGE H. (1960) (ed.) *Tropical Africa*, New York: Twentieth Century.

KRAPF-ASKARI, EVA (1969) *Yoruba Towns and Cities*, Oxford: Clarendon Press.

KUPER, LEO (1967) 'Structural Discontinuities in African Towns: Some Aspects of Racial Pluralism', in Horace Miner (ed.), *The City in Modern Africa*, New York: Praeger.

LA FONTAINE, J. S. (1970) *City Politics: A Study of Leopoldville, 1962/3*, Cambridge University Press.

LESLIE, J. A. K. (1963) *A Social Survey of Dar-es-Salaam*, London: Oxford University Press.

LITTLE, KENNETH (1950) 'The significance of the West African Creole for Africanist and Afro-American studies', *African Affairs*, 49.

LITTLE, KENNETH (1952) *Race and Society*, Paris: UNESCO.

LITTLE, KENNETH (1953) 'The study of "social change" in British West Africa', *Africa*, XXIII (4).

LITTLE, KENNETH (1955a) 'Structural change in the Sierra Leone Protectorate', *Africa*, XXV (3).

LITTLE, KENNETH (1955b) 'The African Elite in British West Africa', in A. W. Lind (ed.), *Race Relations in World Perspective*, Honolulu: University of Hawaii Press.

LITTLE, KENNETH (1965) *West African Urbanization: A Study of Voluntary Associations in Social Change*, Cambridge University Press.

LITTLE, KENNETH (1965–6) 'The political function of the Poro', *Africa*, XXXV, XXXVI (4, 5).

LITTLE, KENNETH (1967a) 'Voluntary Associations in Urban Life: A Case Study of Differential Adaption', in Maurice Freedman (ed.), *Essays presented to Raymond Firth*, London: Cass.

LITTLE, KENNETH (1967b) *The Mende of Sierra Leone*, London: Routledge & Kegan Paul.

LITTLE, KENNETH (1972) 'Some Aspects of African Urbanization South of the Sahara', in *Current Topics in Anthropology*, Reading, Mass.: Addison-Wesley.

LITTLE, KENNETH (1973a) *African Women in Towns: An Aspect of Africa's Social Revolution*, Cambridge University Press.

LITTLE, KENNETH, (1973b) 'Regional Associations: Their Paradoxical Function', in A. W. Southall (ed.), *Urban Anthropology*, London: Oxford University Press.

LITTLE, KENNETH and PRICE, ANNE (1974) *Urbanization, Migration and the African Family* (Module), Reading, Mass.: Addison-Wesley.

LLOYD, P. C. (1966) (ed.) *New Elites of Tropical Africa*, London: Oxford University Press for International African Institute.

LLOYD, P. C. (1967) 'The Elite', in P. C. Lloyd, A. L. Mabogunje and B. Awe (eds), *The City of Ibadan*, Cambridge University Press in association with The Institute of African Studies, Ibadan University.

MABOGUNJE, AKIN L. (1967) 'The Morphology of Ibadan', in P. C. Lloyd, A. L. Mabogunje and B. Awe (eds), *The City of Ibadan*, Cambridge University Press in association with The Institute of African Studies, Ibadan University.

MCQUEEN, ALBERT J. (1969) 'Unemployment of Nigerian school leavers', *Canadian Journal of African Studies*, 3(2).

MANDEVILLE, ELIZABETH (n.d.) unpublished study of Kampala.

MARRIS, PETER (1961) *Family and Social Change in an African City*, London: Routledge & Kegan Paul.

MAYER, PHILIP (1961) *Townsmen or Tribesmen: Conservation and the Process of Urbanization in a South African City*, London: Oxford University Press.

MAZRUI, ALI A. (1963) 'On the concept of "We are all Africans"', *American Political Science Review*, LVII.

MERCIER, PAUL (1955) 'The European community of Dakar', *Cahiers Internationaux de Sociologie*, 19.

MITCHELL, J. CLYDE (1956) *The Kalela Dance, Rhodes-Livingstone Papers*, 27, Manchester University Press for the Institute for Social Research, University of Zambia, reprinted 1968.

MITCHELL, J. CLYDE (1961) 'The Causes of Labour Migration', in Commission for Technical Co-operation in Africa, *Migrant Labour in Africa South of the Sahara*, publication 79.

MITCHELL, J. CLYDE (1962) 'Wage Labour and African Population Movements in Central Africa', in K. M. Barbour and P. M. Prothero (eds), *Essays on African Population*, New York: Praeger.

135

K

MITCHELL, J. CLYDE, and EPSTEIN, A. L. (1959) 'Occupational prestige and social status among the Africans in Northern Rhodesia', *Africa*, XXXIX (1).

MITCHELL, J. CLYDE, and SHAUL, J. R. H. (1965) 'An Approach to the Measurement of Commitment to Urban Residence', in George J. Snowball (ed.), *Science and Medicine in Central Africa*, Oxford: Pergamon Press.

MORRIS, H. STEPHEN (1956) 'Indians in East Africa: a study in plural society', *British Journal of Sociology*, 70 (3).

MORRIS, H. STEPHEN (1957) 'The plural society', *Man*, 57.

MUMFORD, W. B. (1936) *Africans Learn to be French*, London: Evans.

MURUWAH, K. (1938) *Nahnu fi Hriqiyah*, Beirut.

NADEL, S. F. (1942) *A Black Byzantium*, London: Oxford University Press.

NATIONAL STATISTICAL OFFICE, MALAWI (1967) *Annual Survey of Economic Activities*.

NATIONAL STATISTICAL OFFICE, MALAWI (1969) *Reported Employment and Earnings*, Quarterly Report, Third Quarter.

NKRUMAH, KWAME (1965) *Neo-Colonialism: The Last Stage of Imperialism*, London: Nelson.

O'BRIEN, RITA CRUISE (1972) *White Society in Black Africa*, London: Faber.

OFFODILE, E. P. O. (1947) 'Growth and influence of tribal unions', *West African Review*, XVIII (239).

OKEDIJI, F. O. (1967) 'Some social psychological aspects of fertility among married women in an African city (Ibadan)', *Nigerian Journal of Economic and Social Studies*, 9 (1).

OKEDIJI, F. O. and OLADEJO (1966) 'Marital stability and social structure in an African city', *Nigerian Journal of Economic and Social Studies*, 8 (1).

OKEDIJI, F. O., and OPEYEMI, OLA (1967) 'The formation of new élites of tropical Africa', *Odu, University of Ife Journal of African Studies*, 83.

OLIVER, ROLAND, and ATMORE, ANTHONY (1967) *Africa since 1800*, Cambridge University Press.

OLUSANYA, G. O. (1973) *The Second World War and Politics in Nigeria, 1939–1953*, University of Lagos Press.

OPPONG, CHRISTINE (1974) *Marriage among a Matrilineal Elite*, Cambridge University Press.

OTTENBERG, S. (1955) 'Improvement associations among the Afikpo Ibo', *Africa*, XXV (1).

OUSMANE, SEMBENE (1960) *God's Bits of Wood*, London: Heinemann.

OYONO, FERDINAND (1960) *Houseboy*, London: Heinemann.

PADEN, JOHN N. (1970) 'Urban Pluralism, Integration, and Adaption of Communal Identity in Kano, Nigeria', in Ronald Cohen and John Middleton (eds), *From Tribe to Nation in Africa*, Scranton, Pennsylvania: Chandler.

PARKIN, DAVID (1966a) 'Types of African marriage in Kampala', *Africa*, XXVI (3).

PARKIN, DAVID (1966b) 'Voluntary associations as institutions of adaptation', *Man*, 1 (N.S.) (1).

PARKIN, DAVID (1969) *Neighbours and Nationals in an African City Ward*, London: Routledge & Kegan Paul.

PARRINDER, GEOFFREY (1953) *Religion in an African City*, London: Oxford University Press.

PEIL, MARGARET (1965) 'Ghanaian university students: the broadening base', *British Journal of Sociology*, 16 (1).

PEIL, MARGARET (1966) 'Middle school-leavers: occupational aspirations and prospects', *Ghana Journal of Sociology*, 2 (1).

PEIL, MARGARET (1968) 'Aspirations and social structure: a West African example (Ghana)', *Africa*, XXXVIII (1).

PEIL, MARGARET (1972) *The Ghanaian Factory Worker – Industrial Man in Africa*, Cambridge University Press.

PERKIN, HAROLD (1969) *The Origins of Modern English Society, 1780–1880*, London: Routledge & Kegan Paul.

PLOTNICOV, LEONARD (1964) *Modern urban population formation in Nigeria*, paper presented at the Annual Meeting of the American Anthropological Association, Detroit.

PLOTNICOV, LEONARD (1967) *Strangers to the City: Urban Man in Jos, Nigeria*, University of Pittsburgh Press.

PLOTNICOV, LEONARD (1970) 'The Modern African Elite in Jos, Nigeria', in Arthur Tuden and Leonard Plotnicov (eds), *Social Stratification in Africa*, New York: Free Press.

PONS, VALDO (1969) *Stanleyville: An African Urban Community under Belgian Administration*, London: Oxford University Press.

PORTER, ARTHUR (1963) *Creoledom*, Cambridge University Press.

PROUDFOOT, L. and WILSON, H. S. (1961) 'The clubs in crisis: race relations in the new West Africa', *American Journal of Sociology*, LXVI (4).

READ, MARGARET (1942) 'Migrant labour in Africa, and its effects on tribal life', *International Labour Review*, XLV (6).

REISS, ALBERT J., JNR (1964) 'Urbanization', in J. Gould and W. L. Koeb (eds), *A Dictionary of the Social Sciences*, London: Tavistock.

RICHARDS, AUDREY I. (1953) (ed.) *Economic Development and Tribal Change*, Cambridge: Heffer.

ROBERTSON, A. F. (1971) 'African and European social clubs in rural Ghana' *Race*, XII July-April.

ROUCH, JEAN (1954) *Migration in the Gold Coast* (English translation), Accra. Mimeographed.

SASNETT, MARLENE, and SEMPEYER, INEZ (1966) *Educational Systems of Africa*, Berkeley: University of California Press.

SCHAPERA, I. (1947) *Migrant Labour and Tribal Life*, London: Oxford University Press.

SCHWAB, WILLIAM B. (1961) 'Social Stratification in Gwelo', in A. W.

K*

Southall (ed.), *Social Change in Modern Africa*, London: Oxford University Press for International African Institute.

SCHWAB, WILLIAM B. (1965) 'Oshogbo – an Urban Community', in Hilda Kuper (ed.), *Urbanization and Migration in West Africa*, Berkeley: University of California Press.

SIMONS, H. J. and R. E. (1969) *Class and Colour in South Africa 1850–1950*, London: Penguin.

SKINNER, ELLIOTT P. (1965) 'Labour Migration among the Mossi of the Upper Volta', in Hilda Kuper (ed.), *Urbanization and Migration in West Africa*, Berkeley: University of California Press.

SMITH, J. NOEL (1963) 'The Presbyterian Church of Ghana, 1835–1960', unpublished PhD thesis, Edinburgh University.

SMYTHE, HUGH and MABEL (1960) *The New Nigerian Elite*, Stanford University Press.

SOFER, CYRIL (1954) 'Working groups in a plural society', *Industrial and Labour Relations Review*, 8.

SOFER, CYRIL (1956) 'Urban African Social Structure and Working Group Behaviour at Jinja (Uganda)', in *Social Aspects of Urbanization and Industrialization in Africa*, Paris: UNESCO.

SOFER, CYRIL and RHONA (1955) *Jinja Transformed*, East African Studies, no. 4, Kampala: East African Institute of Social Research.

SOUTHALL, A. W. (1954) 'Alur Migrants', in Audrey T. Richards (ed.), *Economic Development and Tribal Change*, Cambridge: Heffer.

SOUTHALL, A. W. (1961) Introductory Summary in A. W. Southall (ed.), *Social Change in Modern Africa*, London: Oxford University Press for International African Institute.

SOUTHALL, A. W., and GUTKIND, PETER C. W. (1957) *Townsmen in the Making*, Kampala: East African Institute of Social Research.

STANLEY, WILLIAM R. (1970) 'The Lebanese in Sierra Leone', *African Urban Notes*, V (2).

STEEL, R. W. (1961) 'The Towns of Tropical Africa', in K. M. Barbour and R. M. Prothero (eds), *Essays on African Population*, London: Routledge & Kegan Paul.

SUNDKLER, B. (1961) *Bantu Prophets in South Africa*, London: Oxford University Press for International African Institute.

TIWARI, R. C. (1972) 'Some aspects of the social geography of Nairobi, Kenya', *African Urban Notes*, V (2).

UNITED NATIONS ECONOMIC COMMISSION FOR AFRICA (UNECA) (1962) 'Introduction to the Problems of Urbanization in Tropical Africa', in *Workshop on Urbanization in Africa*, Addis Ababa.

VAN DEN BERGHE, PIERRE (1969) 'Some social characteristics of University of Ibadan students', *Nigerian Journal of Economics and Social Science*, II, 3.

VAN DER HORST, SHEILA (1965) 'The Effects of Industrialization on Race Relations in South Africa', in Guy Hunter (ed.), *Industrialization and Race Relations*, London: Oxford University Press for Institute of Race Relations.

VAN VELSEN, J. (1961) 'Labour Migration as a Positive Factor in the

Continuity of Tonga Tribal Society', in A. W. Southall (ed.), *Social Change in Modern Africa*, London: Oxford University Press for International African Institute.

WALLERSTEIN, IMMANUEL (1960) 'Ethnicity and national integration', *Cahiers d'Etudes Africaines*, 3.

WHEATLEY, PAUL (1970) 'The significance of traditional Yoruba urbanism', *Comparative Studies in Society and History*, 12.

WILSON, GODFREY (1941–2) *An Essay on the Economics of De-tribalization*, Rhodes-Livingstone Institute, Papers 5 and 6.

WINDER, R. BAYLEY (1961–2) 'The Lebanese in West Africa', *Comparative Studies in Society and History*, 4.

WIRTH, LOUIS (1938) 'Urbanism as a way of life', *American Journal of Sociology*, XLIV (8).

WOBER, MALLORY (1967) 'Individualism, home life and work efficiency among a group of Nigerian workers', *Occupational Psychology*, XLI.

WOBER, MALLORY (1971) 'The concept of job satisfaction among workers in particular in a Nigerian industry', *International Review of Applied Psychology*, 20 (1).

WYNDHAM, H. A. (1935) *The Atlantic and Slavery*, London: Oxford University Press.

Index

importance of, 102;
socio-economic strata in, 44–5
civil servants: education and, 45–6;
European colonial, 56; home
backgrounds of, 28–9; illiteracy
percentages of parents and
grandparents, 28–9; income of,
41, 42; percentage of, in Accra, 41;
socio-economic rating, 44–5
civil service: Africanization of, 27–8;
Creoles in, 25, 26; évolués in, 25,
26, 45; expansion under
Independence, 26–7; Ghanaian,
27–8; Nigerian, 27, 28;
opportunities for employment in,
26; percentage of posts held by
Africans, 27, 28, 113
civilized way of life: African view of,
46–7; wage-employment and, 57–8;
Western view of, 96–8
class, see social class
clerks: Africans as government, 25;
incomes of, 42; and the
intelligentsia, 35, 48; job-satisfaction
levels, 35; social status of, 45
clothes: possession of, as 'civilized',
46; purchase of, by migrants, 14;
of upper income groups, 42, 43
clubs: exclusive European, 56, 120;
membership according to status
57; membership and race relations,
65, 120; quasi-traditional nature
of, 98
colonialism, race relations under,
56–60
commerce, commercial: business
establishments in cities, 11;
interests of regional associations,
92; international, and urbanization,
101–2; need for educated personnel,
57; and the origin of African
cities, 97; percentage of directors
and managers in cities, 41; race
relations and, 57–8
compins: dancing, 89, 126; linking
traditional and urban ways, 89–90;
membership of, 126; purpose of,
89; Temne, 94, 126
Congo: Belgian government policy,
29; Belgian migration policy, 15–16,
17; demographic data, 108;
political career of 'new men',
29–30; university education in, 27

Congo Republic, higher education
in, 27
Copper Belt: administrative and
economic arrangements, 75;
categorization in, 75–6; cities of,
22, 24; ethnicity in, 75; migrant
residence in, 33; migration to, 18;
mobility of population, 75; social
organization of, 74–81;
urbanization in, 74–5
Creoles: educational standards of,
25, 113; origin of, 25; role in
government, 25, 26
culture, cultural: diversity in Copper
Belt, 75; heterogeneity in cities, 23,
96; migrants retaining traditional,
50–2; role of Creoles, Cape
Coloured group, and évolués, 25;
separation, British and African,
64–5; similarity and categorization,
75–6; and social differences in
Francophone countries, 59–60
currency: European, 8, 10; native, 10

Dahomey: demographic data, 20,
108; foreign aid to, 102
Dakar: demographic data, 110;
évolués of, 25; influx of French
population, 59; racial separation
and antagonism, 59–60; rise of, 8;
university of, 27
dancing: attitudes to women, 38;
compins, 89, 126
Dar es Salaam: demographic data,
110; as a modern city, 24;
regional association, 90
Deima, 87
demographic: data, official sources
of, 112; data of African cities, 7,
8, 108–10; factors as criterion of
city, 22; features of modern cities,
24, 96; meanings of urbanization,
4, 5–6
divorce rates, 98, 126
doctors, 41, 56, 90

East Africa: attitudes to migration,
17–18; credit associations, 88;
Indian migration to, 10
East London, Xhosa migrants in,
18, 38
economic, economy: dependence on
foreign finance, 102; development

147